Goddess Liberated

Feminine Love & Empowerment
in a post-patriarchal World

Ariadne Ross

Goddess Liberated

Feminine Love
& Empowerment
in a post-patriarchal World

ARIADNE ROSS

Göttin Press

www.goddessliberated.info

Cover Design: Anna Hasenaka, Illustrator/Artist

ISBN-13: 978-0-9904688-4-4

Library of Congress Control Number: 2014910354

Published by
Göttin Press, Nahant, Massachusetts
www.goettin.info

to my sisters

Goddess Liberated

CONTENTS

Goddess Liberated

ILLUSTRATIONS

Goddess Liberated

Preface

(which you really should read)

This is a book fundamentally about physics, but it is decidedly not a physics book. This is a feminist book about embracing and celebrating the Feminine. This is a book about Love, and about Truth. This is a book about quantum reality as the basis of our lives, manifesting in our lives every moment of every day, whether we want it to or not. This is a book about free will and freedom. You may choose to reject free will, but that means you reject the reality of the universe itself. This is a book about Goddess. It is an atheist book, an atheism that means total individual responsibility for our actions, or our inaction. This book is decidedly anti-patriarchy, anti-religious, and anti-capitalist. This book takes a mostly dim view of the "new age" for reasons which will be explained, but acknowledges that some thinkers associated with the "new age" at least started out on the right track. In fact, this is in many ways a "how to" book: how to smash patriarchy and rid it from your life, how to embrace the Feminine, how to harness your true creative power. This is also a "how things work" book: how the universe works at a quantum level, physically and metaphysically. This is a book about healing the earth-plane and healing Gaia before humanity has the chance to complete Gaia's, and thus our own, imminent destruction. Nevertheless this really *is* a book about having fun, not taking things too seriously, taking risks, doing what is right, and in short, just saying "Fuck It!"

Is this a work of fiction or non-fiction? This book builds upon deeply honest and introspective "conversations" I've had with my own true self – not verbal "conversations," but thought conversations transcribed into verbal form as best as I've been able to capture the original non-verbal conversational thought. Are your own deeply honest and introspective thoughts non-fiction, or fictional? If you'd argue for the latter, I invite you to read this book with an open mind and feel if it resonates with your own true feelings. If you truly feel the former is true, I invite you to read this book with an open mind and feel if it resonates with your own true feelings. Either way, the fact that you have gotten as far as reading this book and this preface means you somehow got yourself to this point – not via any religious or pseudo-religious process, or through a "poof!" of divine revelation, but I also contend you didn't get here as a result of purely random "white noise" either (if you lived your life that way, you'd have been dead long before now).

This book is very much about your interactions with the quantum processes and connections, i.e. the physics, that got you to this point, that are keeping you where you are, and that will get you to where you are going. Some of these are fairly simple, others quite complex, but if you think about the way these quantum processes and connections work, just as with biological evolution, the reality is far more fascinating and astounding than any disempowering patriarchal religious tenet ever could be. And just as with biological evolution (or global warming), ignoring quantum reality doesn't make it go away. So is this book really based on physics, or metaphysics (at least when metaphysics is understood from an atheist perspective)? I say there really is no difference at a quantum level – which this book argues *is the only level* at which reality happens - and whether through the well documented double-slit experiment or more recent research verifying delayed-choice entanglement or retrocausality at even a macroscopic level, the difference between physics and metaphysics is really semantic. Quantum processes are probabilistic but not random. If you find yourself thinking "huh...?" at this point, please don't despair and for now pretend you didn't even read this paragraph. I hope the "how things work" parts of this book will shed some light, and I've suggested some references which I've found helpful for beginning to understand these concepts. And remember, just as organisms don't need to know how to evolve in order to evolve, and you don't need to know how an airplane works to fly in one, and you don't need to know how it is that humans can ride a bicycle (not actually easy!) in order to ride one, you don't need to understand the "how things work" aspects of this book in order to apply the principles described in this book. In fact, you are already perfectly equipped to do this!

Some final pointers before you read this book:

- Go ahead and read it, what have you got to lose?

- If you do go ahead and read this book, *be forewarned*: you cannot un-know what you read here

- Approach this book with a dry sense of humor and you'll understand it (and me) much better

- Portions, large parts, the entirety, or even the very title of this book might piss you off. If that's the case, (a) I really don't care, and (b) please re-read the preceding bullet

- Feel free to read this book out of order – I certainly wrote it that way – but it might be clearer if you read it mostly in order the first time through

- If you are reading this book to be mean, to bully, to harass, to better cozy up to and be coddled by patriarchy – then fuck off

- If you are reading this book to think freer, to be freer, to help others and help the earth, to embrace your immense creative power, then enjoy – and just say "Fuck It!"

Ariadne Ross
June 2014

Goddess Liberated

Goddess Liberated

Chapter 1

Patriarchy:
a fish rots from the head[*]

A (possibly, hopefully) fixable mess

We are in deep trouble. This is nothing new, but on balance the explosive rate at which the mess has been worsening should be of deepening concern to all of us. And the situation *is* serious. If you haven't noticed how much trouble we're in, or even had an inkling that things are dreadfully amiss, then I am especially happy you've found this book. I hope you read this book with an open mind, and most of all with an open heart.

Who is the "we" who are in deep trouble? Each and all of us. And when I say "all of us" I don't mean just us humans inhabiting earth, but the multitude of life that constitute the system that is Gaia. And by "life" I don't just mean those life

---

[*] This is a widespread proverb of unknown origin. A fish doesn't actually rot from the head first; this is a metaphor.

forms currently accepted as such by most of the scientific community, but everyone and everything that comprehends Gaia: Her rocks and minerals, Her atmosphere, Her land surface, Her oceans of course, as well as all the life forms that dwell in one or more of these realms – including humans. This book is directed at humans not because they are the ones "smart enough" to read the language of this book, nor because they are somehow "above" the rest of Gaia in any way whatsoever, but because they are the only species stupid enough to have gotten Gaia into this mess, yet still (possibly, hopefully) smart enough to get Her out of it. What's worse, while humans have occasionally just bumbled into earth-destruction, more often than not their attacks on Gaia have been willful and coordinated. For humans, it is a matter of responsibility to do all they can to fix things, and fix them fast.

I promise this first chapter will be the darkest of the book but it is important we embark from a position of realism rather than denial, and form a common understanding of what the mess is and who is causing it so that we can move toward restoring and fixing us and all of Gaia. I want this book to be frank and blunt and hard-hitting, but above all I want the message here to be one of hope, paths to solutions, and love. Yes, the mess *is* huge, the troubles *are* deep, for humans the jig *is* almost up, but despite all of this, there really is hope if enough of us engage our feelings, our intuition, and our creativity to start repairing and reversing the damage we've been doing to Gaia and to each other. We can't begin repairing Gaia without starting to repair ourselves, for we are all inextricably intertwined. The good news is that the quantum universe provides the infrastructure and tools we need to turn things around – we only have to use this infrastructure and these tools for *con*structive rather than *de*structive purposes. The great news is that there is no god nor are there any god-like beings whom we can beseech for help. It is us and us alone who are empowered, with all of our free will at our disposal, and we can begin making things right, immediately. Certainly, we cannot fix the mess alone, but the other good news is that the very quantum nature of the universe means we don't have to get everyone, or even a majority, on board in order to get the repairs underway. Make no mistake, we are talking about a revolution here, but a revolution in which our inter-connectedness makes our "baby steps" have every bit the impact as do the rarer occasions of "sea change".

Never doubt that every kindness we engage in with one another or any part of Gaia has a far greater impact than you could possibly imagine. Some of how this works and evidence that it *does* work will be addressed in this book. As is the case with any revolution, we just need a small critical number of us to begin making things right with each other and with Gaia, and the physics of the universe ensures the repairs will accelerate just as the destruction had been accelerating. So there truly *is* hope, and a lot of it, even though things are still pretty damn dark overall and the storm continues gathering. Will we be able to truly get repairs underway, begin fixing the mess enough so that we can turn things around? Maybe, maybe not. But we are the ones who have the power and empowerment and free will to pull this off. We might fail, but don't we owe it to ourselves, to each other, to our children, and to all of Gaia to never stop trying?

Humans and all of the earth comprise a unified system, no matter how hard humans try to distance themselves from "the natural world" which is nothing more, nor less, than all of Gaia. To say humans are the only ones "smart enough" to save Gaia from disaster is not really accurate. The system that is Gaia will self-heal one way or another, with humans on the planet or without them. But if we are relying on Gaia's "immune system" to fix things, we won't be here to see the results. While there would be a peculiar irony in seeing the species responsible for a terrestrial extinction rate 10,000 times the natural one[1] themselves become extinct, such *Schadenfreude* is decidedly not the point-of-view of this book. If we humans truly want to do what is right and earnestly begin fixing the mess we've made of things, we have to begin fixing our distinctly human mess just as earnestly and just as urgently.

The imminent threat to humans, by humans, is just as bleak as the situation humans have imposed on Gaia. Well, this does not exactly apply to *all* humans, does it? You probably encounter almost daily (at best in the media, worst case in person) people who could care less that things range from bad to really bad to bleak to destitute for well more than half of earth's human population. These same people are flippantly careless about Gaia's dire state, and she is on life support now. And yet, these very same people are "running" things! How can this be?

Who are they, and why weren't they stopped long ago?

Just the examples of human oppression and pain and suffering would fill a book as substantial as one documenting the destructions afflicting the rest of Gaia, and it is important to document the arrogance of oppression in all of these circumstances, but that is not the main point of this book, which is foremost about hope, and solution, and love. The remainder of this chapter overviews a few chilling but important examples of how bad it is for (almost all) humans, and how dreadful it is for the rest of Gaia. But first, some necessary introductions:

Meet the Feminine! Greet the Goddess! Confront Patriarchy

Chances are very good that if you're reading this book, you are already part of the **Feminine**. You may consciously know you are part of the Feminine, or you may have a general inkling about this, or your Feminine may be deliberately hidden to try and protect you from the onslaught of our oppressors, but it is very likely you are part of the Feminine, and that is absolutely wonderful! I won't spend much time in this chapter defining the Feminine, since much of the rest of this book is about discovering, opening up and developing ourselves in the Feminine. But I do want to point out that when I refer to "Feminine" or "the Feminine" I am not referring to gender and I am not in any way endorsing a gender binary. What I mean by "the Feminine" has very much to do with truth in love, and truth in feeling and intuition, being true to yourself. When I use "Feminine" I am referring to you personally, and by the Feminine" I am referring to the Feminine collective. There are people across the gender spectrum who are Feminine and part of the Feminine. It does happen that on earth today that most, but by no means all, women are Feminine and part of the Feminine, as are most gender-nonconforming and LGBTQ people, and that most, but not all, men are not part of the Feminine (but among those men who are not part of the Feminine, a significant number are Feminine-curious). Again, being part of the Feminine has nothing to do with gender. I don't want to get stuck on the semantic limitations of language, which is really the issue here. Being truly Feminine, it is your absolute nature to help and nurture everyone, regardless of whether they are truly masculine or Feminine, and that is as it should be. If you did not act this way, you would not be truly Feminine. I deliberately avoided any term like "Divine Feminine" since that reeks of some kind of patriarchal binary or worse, religion. That said, in this first chapter and occasionally afterward I do refer to "women" and "female" with some necessary equivalence to Feminine since these are the terms the patriarchal milieu uses to define those of us who are Feminine and part of the Feminine.

If "Feminine" and "the Feminine" are difficult to define, **Goddess** belies any semantic definition at all. Yet all of us *feel* who and what Goddess is, all of us already know Goddess whether or not we consciously realize it, and the concept of

Goddess is absolutely central to this book. Goddess can only be *felt* with true Feeling, but cannot be known in mentality, and therein lies a central problem in trying to define Her. In no way am I implying Goddess is "the opposite" of god (she is not), no more than I am implying the opposite of patriarchy is matriarchy (it is not).

Love has no opposite, but if it did, it would be fear.

For me this is a fundamental truth for feeling Goddess and understanding the Feminine (and we will explore this in depth throughout this book). This is why there is no opposite of Goddess that is god, the two are completely different concepts. Likewise, there is no opposite of Feminine that is masculine, these are completely different concepts. Goddess and the Feminine are anarchic, while patriarchy serves and obeys the archons. The Feminine is love, patriarchy rules by fear.

As far as **patriarchy** is concerned, the rest of this chapter is not so much about defining it as confronting its hideousness and its ugly manifestations head-on in a rogue's gallery kind of way. Neither pretty nor pleasant, but necessary. I couldn't think of a more succinct and superb way to sum up what I mean by patriarchy than the words of esteemed feminist and academic bell hooks: "imperialist white-supremacist capitalist patriarchy".[2] When you read "patriarchy" in this book and you substitute Dr. hooks' words, you will have a vivid definition of patriarchy, including the self-referential part of her phrase.

Humans, we're a mess ...

Patriarchy to the rest of us: "you're our bitch"

Patriarchy owns the world economy, and it is patriarchal economics that is the linchpin of their entire oppressive system. From religion - the always reliable but increasingly irrelevant lapdog of the patriarchal system, to patriarchy's very own perpetual money machine - the military/industrial/research complex US president Eisenhower[§] so gravely warned about over 60 years ago,[3] to governments throughout the world, patriarchy owns it all, and they've established their capitalist economic system to keep it that way. Take just the example of politics in the United States. During the 2012 presidential campaign, $178 million was spent by US corporations, $240 million by super-PACs,[4] $122 million by just 10 individual donors,[5] all totaled $2.3 billion were spent by patriarchy to buy both major party candidates. Despite all of the rhetoric, this spending was evenly divided between both major party candidates, and by corporate sector it was divided just as equally.[6] I guess this is what patriarchy means when they say "win-win".

Patriarchal economic domination, oppression of the

[§] "In the councils of government, we must guard against the acquisition of unwarranted influence, whether sought or unsought, by the military industrial complex. The potential for the disastrous rise of misplaced power exists and will persist. We must never let the weight of this combination endanger our liberties or democratic processes. We should take nothing for granted." - Dwight D. Eisenhower

disenfranchised (i.e. virtually all of us), and blatant economic criminality in the so-called "democracies" of the capitalist so-called "free market economies" is just as endemic as it is in the rest of the world. The rich, super-rich, indescribably super-rich, and just plain unspeakably rich love hierarchy and structure – it is all about being on top - and they are particularly good at shifting attention away from themselves (after all, they have an astounding amount of money at their disposal) - consider the short shrift suppression of the Occupy movement. No matter where you find them, the patriarchy are quite adept at sedating the populace. In the "1st world" it is all about getting you to focus on things and the need for upgrading your things in an endless spiral to nowhere. Mass sports, mass entertainment, mass hatred, objectifying women, any suitable distraction with mass appeal will do, red herrings fed to the masses at every turn. Mixed with the proper dose of fear and subjugation, patriarchy have perfected the drug that morphs people into "sheeple". Aren't there patriarchal structures in the 2nd and 3rd worlds too? Of course there are, they are just further down the patriarchal pyramid (patriarchy loves the pyramid, puts the populace in cubes, and abhors circles).

Consider one of patriarchy's favorite pyramids, the "global wealth pyramid" they love to crow about, and use to compare themselves to one another while lording their monetary wealth and power over 99.6% of the rest of the planet. In 2011 the global rich, about 30 million people worldwide and defined as those with assets of more than US $1 million, were worth an astonishing US $89.1 trillion,[7] owning 38.5% - well over one-third – of the world's money, yet they are only 0.4% of the world's population, about that of Iraq.[8] The numbers for 2013 were even worse. The 85 wealthiest people in the world held a combined wealth of $1.67 trillion (€1.2 trillion), as much as the poorest 3.5 billion people. Yes, *85 people have as much wealth as one-half of the entire world's population.*[9] The super-rich, defined as people with assets of US $30 million or more (not US corporation-people, but actual human-people), number only 187,380, accounting for 0.0026% of the earth's population (about half that of Iceland), yet own US $26 trillion (11% of the world's money). A single US investment firm, BlackRock, managed over $4.4 trillion in assets in 2013, and invested in virtually *every* firm listed on *every* stock market around the world, owning 3% ~ 10% of the assets of *all* of the world's largest corporations.[10] In 2013, BlackRock controlled $1.4 trillion *more* than the US government's revenue![11] On the other hand, the bottom of the wealth pyramid, defined as those with less than US $10,000 in assets, numbered over 3 billion people – 42% of the world's human population – but possessed a *combined* "wealth" that was a mere 3.3% of the world's total. The world's rich, less than 30 million people, less than 1/100th of the 3 billion people at the bottom of the wealth pyramid, have 12 times as much wealth as all of these 3 billion people *combined.* Every year the situation worsens drastically.[¶]

¶   This was a 29% increase from just the prior year! During the same year, the global wealth held by the remaining 99.6% of us was unchanged, but the wealth of the bottom 3 billion people *decreased* by almost 10%.

Like any pimp, patriarchy keeps for themselves almost all of the money their victims earn, begrudgingly giving the exploited just enough to keep them more-or-less placated. €25,000,000,000,000 – that's €25 trillion – has been hoarded away by European Union (EU)-based corporations in offshore tax havens to deprive EU citizens of the money that is theirs,[12] so badly needed to address a host of problems, including unemployment of 27% in Spain and Greece,[13] youth unemployment EU-wide over 23%, led by Greece with 58% and Spain with 55% of people under age 25 unemployed.[14] If these EU-based criminal corporations were to return the money they've stolen back to the citizens of the EU, they could give €50,000 to every single woman, child and man in the EU, enough to buy every citizen a brand new luxury automobile. In the United States, just in the year 2012, 20 large US corporations stashed a mind-boggling $1 trillion in offshore tax havens, avoiding taxes they owe the citizens of their country.[15] Of course this repugnant tax evasion behavior is not limited to corporations (in the US they are known as "people"), the wealthy and super-wealthy do it, too. A recent massive study by the International Committee of Investigative Journalists (ICIJ) uncovered 130,000 people from 170 countries stashing US $32 trillion in offshore tax havens out of the reach of the exploited.[16] Despite extensive coverage in German and French[17] media, the findings of the ICIJ have (of course) merited barely a whisper in the english-language press.

Of course, patriarchy wouldn't be patriarchy if there weren't levels of hierarchy everywhere, and that includes within the monied elite (which is identical to the patriarchal elite, since the patriarchal pyramid always ends up being about monetary wealth). In terms of race and geography, there is patriarchy, and then there is *patriarchy*. It's much like membership in the United States' ultra-patriarchal, ultra-elite Augusta National Golf Club, home of the Masters tournament. Until 1982, all of the caddies were required to be black, no black was allowed to join the club until 1990 (there are reportedly "a handful" today), and the first two women were allowed to join only in 2012 (one of whom is Condoleeza Rice, a black woman).[18] North America leads the ultra-rich patriarchy with 34% of the ultra-wealthy's wealth, which when combined with Europe's 27% makes 61% of the world's ultra-wealthy also ultra-white. Africa's super-wealthy, despite the continent's 1.3 billion people, held a puny 1% of the world's money (numbers for how many of these super-rich Africans are also white were not available).[19] The 1st world's patriarchy are the overlords of the 2nd and 3rd world patriarchies, who in turn exploit their own populations for the aggrandizement of the patriarchal pyramid, with the subjects of the 2nd and 3rd world patriarchs suffering a bit more subjugation and repression than their 1st world counterparts, but on balance, patriarchy is patriarchy, their methods merely different flavors of the same bane.

Keep the women out! (of power)

Women, children and other marginalized members of the masses suffer greatly and disproportionately at the hands of patriarchy, of course. This is deliberate, patriarchy runs the show, and they are hell bent on keeping it that way. Important as it is for them to keep women, the oppressed and marginalized out of politics and higher education, patriarchy must keep the priesthood of capitalism purely filthy, and its holy of holies - money and economics – unclean. In short, keep the Feminine out at all costs. Let's face it, if women and all of the marginalized ran the economy, they would soon be running governments, and then patriarchal capitalism would be vanquished from the planet, people would be treated equitably for the first time in many thousand years, they would be well fed and well nurtured and happy ... there is no way patriarchy intends to allow such a Feminine revolution to even come close to taking place! So here are just a few examples of the way patriarchy keep their system of power, enslavement, exploitation, and pacification humming along. When you consider just some of the devastation patriarchy has already wrought, and just get an inkling of feeling the suffering that *all* of Gaia have felt under patriarchal tyranny, could you reach any other conclusion than it is time to take immediate action, restore the Feminine, and take our planet back? And that the only way to do this is to excise patriarchy, and do it now?

Women are severely underrepresented in national legislatures worldwide, and predictably representation is worst in the centers of patriarchal money and power. In the world's top 20 countries for Gross Domestic Product (GDP), accounting for 80% of total world GDP, average representation for women in parliament is a mere 22.7% (and it's even worse for the top 10 GDP countries, which combined have 65% of world GDP, but only 19.6% of their legislators are women). Contrast that with the top 20 countries for female parliamentary representation, averaging 41.8% women in their legislatures, but a combined GDP of only 7.4% of the world.[20] The top 10 countries for female legislative representation with an average of 45% women in parliament come reasonably close to parity, but together these 10 countries account for a meager 1.6% of world GDP.[§] Among the big 5 economic powers, the United States ranks a dismal 78th in women in legislature (less than 18%, below Saudi Arabia), Russia 98th (under 14% women), India 109th where only 11% of parliamentarians are women, and Japan an abysmal 123rd with a mere 8% of legislators being female.[21]

It is one thing to allow a few women into politics, but to give them any real control over the capitalist economy is unthinkable. It is fine to exploit them - women make up 50% of the worldwide workforce -[22] yet less than 20% of companies have any women in executive positions, and they account for only 14% of "Fortune 500" corporate board positions, with more than 25%

---

§ The top 10 countries for female representation are (in ranking order) Rwanda, Andorra, Cuba, Sweden, Seychelles, Senegal, Finland, South Africa, and Nicaragua).

of corporations having no women executives at all. Even worse, women represent only 4% of CEOs (Chief Executive Officers) of the largest 1000 companies in the world.[23] Despite half a century of legislated pay equity, whether you are a woman in Germany,[24] the United Kingdom,[25] or the United States[26] you still earn 20% less than your male counterpart. I guess this is not surprising when you consider the vast differences between even the perceptions of sexism and sexual harassment between men and women. In a 2013 German television survey, 89% of women said there is a sexism problem in Germany, but only 15% of German men thought there was any problem.[27] And don't forget how much patriarchy love their pyramid. Kicking their subjects at the bottom while keeping the downtrodden in competition with each other for the meager leavings from the patriarchal table is a favorite bloodsport of theirs. I guess white women are supposed to feel fortunate to earn 80% of their male colleagues. The average black man in the US earns just 75% of his white male counterpart, but the average black woman less than 70% of a white man in the same job. Hispanic women in the United States fare worst of all among defined groups, earning under $0.60 for every $1.00 earned by a white man in the same job.[28] In the United States, the number of single-parent families has climbed to 1 in 3, in the UK 1 in 4, and France and Germany 1 in 5 families have children being raised by a single parent.[29] But whether in the US,[30] UK,[31] or Germany,[32] *90% of single parent families are headed by women,* 30% of these families live in poverty,[33] and at least half of the women heading single-parent families are unable to be in the workforce due to the inability to find affordable, adequate, stable child care.[34,35]

Let the women in! (to be raped and abused)

Consider just some examples of the criminal abuse of women and children under patriarchal tyranny, and the facts of how bad it is speak for themselves:

- A recent study by the International Labor Organization (ILO) found that 21 million people are slaves in the year 2014, the vast majority of them women and children. The enslaved make $150 billion in profits for their capitalist owners, $99 billion of which comes from forced prostitution[36]

- A major study by the World Health Organization in 2013 found that *35% of women worldwide over 15 years old have suffered physical and/or sexual violence* - more than 1 of every 3 women.[37]

- In the most recent United Kingdom Ministry of Justice study, 76% of those convicted of crimes and sentenced were men.[38]

- In the United States, men accounted for 85% of murderers[39] and 99% of rapists.[40] One-in-five women (20%) in the United States *report* being raped,[41] but the actual number is much worse since over 50% of rape cases in the US are unreported.[42]

- During the 100-day Rwandan genocide (see section below), an estimated 500,000 women were raped (resulting in 20,000 pregnancies from rape), and of the survivors 2 out of every 3 were infected with HIV/AIDS.[43]

- In just the first four months of 2013, there were 1822 rapes reported to authorities in Rio de Janeiro, but only 70 arrests in connection with these rapes – a mere 5% of the reported rape cases.[44]

- On Wednesday, 3 July 2013, while Egyptians rallied against patriarchy on Tahrir Square, over 80 women were subjected to rape and mob sexual violence that day alone.[45]

- In Pakistan, 90% of women are subjected to sexual violence, and more than 1000 women per year are murdered in so-called "honor killings". Acid attacks against women at the hands of jilted male suitors are horrific and commonplace in Pakistan, which has been named the "world's worst country for women and girls."[46]

- In 2001 Germany passed a feminist-sponsored, well-intentioned law legalizing prostitution, envisioning prostitutes working "freely, insured, happy with their work, well paid and paying taxes." Patriarchy could not stand for this dignity, of course - the reality in Germany today is a horror scenario where pimps reign with impunity, 90% of prostitutes work against their will, about 80% arriving from economically depressed eastern European countries (primarily Rumania and Bulgaria). There are now over 200,000 prostitutes working in Germany. When one brothel opened in Stuttgart, police reported "busloads of customers arriving from very far away" and local papers said "700 men were waiting in line" to enter the bordello. A typical brothel advertisement promises "Sex with any women as long as you want, as often as you want, and how you want. Sex. Anal sex. Oral sex (without a condom). Threesome. Group sex. Gang bang. €70 daytime, €100 evenings." These young women earn virtually nothing, being forced to give up their clothes, forced to work 18+ hours a day for men juiced up on drugs for "erectile dysfunction", forced in their few off hours sleeping three women to a bed, prohibited from leaving the premises, and for these privileges they typically must pay their pimps €800 per week. If these women fail to perform, or are simply "not nice enough" to customers, they are often beaten, stabbed, or worse.[47]

- At first look Putian, China seems like the idyllic seaside city a tourist agency might use to showcase the remaining traditional aspects of China. Meizhou Island just offshore is, ironically, best known as the birthplace of the Goddess Matsu, the Chinese sea goddess. Ironic, because Putian's real distinction is dubious and tragic: it features a beach from which more Chinese families set out and drown their baby girls at sea than anywhere else in China; only male children are deemed useful in this largely fishing-industry city. But Putian's tragic distinction does not stop there. If a baby girl is fortunate enough to survive past her neonatal month, lucky enough to have a loving family, there is a very good chance her life will be destroyed anyway. Just since 2007, more than 20,000 girls have been kidnapped from Putian – walking to or from school, off of the school playground, and even from the very room at home where they sleep – kidnapped and sold to be brides in one of China's many "bachelor cities", fetching a grand price of about €12 (but through a macabre after market, she might be re-sold for as much as €100). For modern times this is a rare occasion where we know the actual numeric value patriarchy places on a woman. As a side-effect of China's one-child policy, there are now 37 million more men than women in China, and the differential is growing dramatically. For every 4 Chinese girls, there are 5 boys. Many rural cities and towns have no girls at all. Locals say "the only place you'll find a girl is on a billboard." The kidnapped girls are forced to become wives, but almost all have no idea who their parents were, where they came from, or even how old they are. In the words of a major Chinese human rights organization, "the government is terrified that the outside world will find out the magnitude of this problem in China. The Party does not want to lose face." They estimate, conservatively, that 550 young girls are sold in China every day.[48,49]

The examples could sadly go on and on, and on. What does it say about patriarchy when they've engineered a system where a woman in the world's wealthiest country is 500% more likely to be a rape victim in her lifetime than to be a corporate executive or member of parliament? Or when seemingly the only hope for a woman to get out of utter economic depression is to sell her body into slavery to patriarchy? Or when the price of a girl's life, if she isn't murdered first, is €12.

Patriarchy: Ultimate Killing Machine

Genocide statistics are staggering, so staggering the numbers seem surreal. An estimated 170,000,000 people were murdered by other people during the 20th century's many genocides, compared to approximately 36,000,000 direct combat deaths.[50] You only need to go back to the latter 20th century to find mass killings of humans by humans. From 1975 through 1979, 1,700,000 Cambodians lost their lives at the hands of their own government, nearly 1/4th of the population (and this after suffering 231,000 aerial bombing raids dropping 2.7 million tons of bombs by US forces during the Vietnam war).[51] The US, China, and Russia, so keenly involved in the region in the previous years during that just-ended Vietnam war, stood by and did nothing.

In 1994, a three-way religious war raged in the Balkans killing over 200,000 civilians. After initial hope, it was clear the world's powerful countries were going to do pretty much nothing to stop it.[52] Simultaneously during a 100 day period in 1994, nearly 2,000,000 Rwandans were slaughtered by their fellow Rwandans in an ethnic genocide.[53] The world's powerful nations stood by and did absolutely nothing – and worse, it has been proven the United States knew what was about to happen in advance, and deliberately chose to do nothing.[54] In consecutive civil wars between 1996 and 2003, about 5,000,000 Congolese were slaughtered in the Democratic Republic of Congo.[¶] The world's economic and military powers stood by and watched.[55] Meanwhile during their 22 year civil war (1983~2005) an estimated 2,000,000 Sudanese civilians lost their lives, either due to direct military attack or deliberate genocidal mass starvation.[56]

Now consider Iraq and Afghanistan. From 2003~2010, without hesitation, the United States and its allies invaded and occupied Iraq at a cost of US $3.9 trillion.[57] At least 134,000 Iraqi civilians have died as a direct result of the invasion, war, and its consequences, and an additional 52,000 people "directly involved" (including military, police, and government contractors) also perished in the war and occupation.[58] When the costs of the Afghanistan war (also launched without hesitation)

¶   That still doesn't come close to the 10,000,000 Congolese killed during the Belgian occupation of the late 19th and early 20th centuries, all in exchange for rubber, that era's oil.

are added in, the total costs of both wars to the United States alone is $6,000,000,000,000 ($6 trillion), or about $75,000 for each woman, child, and man in the United States. The estimated cost to the United Kingdom is £7.4 billion but probably much larger than that.[59] The US cost alone makes the Iraq/Afghanistan Wars the (monetarily) costliest conflicts in world history.[60]

What is it about Iraq and Afghanistan that make them so very special to warrant such incredible attention from the most powerful nations on earth and their subsidiaries? Based on all prior behavior by the rich and powerful nations, it cannot be the magnitude of the genocides there. True, both countries were suffering under despotic regimes or religious extremism, and the 50,000+ people estimated killed by Saddam Hussein is horrific,[61] but that number pales in comparison to the 11,000,000 killed in just the handful of genocides discussed above (and also pales in comparison to the civilian deaths after the US and its allies "liberated" those countries). And it can't be those two countries' GDP, which together amount to a scant 0.18% of world GDP. Nor can it be the populations of Iraq and Afghanistan, which combined is 60 million, much less than the 72 million of the DR Congo alone, and far less than the 146 million who live in the small group of genocide countries discussed in this book.[†] Clearly, something else must be the source of the United States', Britain's, and more recently, China's[62] passion about Iraq and Afghanistan. You don't have to look far to find the answer.

---

† The populations of Cambodia, the DR Congo, Rwanda and Sudan would be considerably higher if it weren't for the genocides; in each of these the populations have still not recovered from pre-genocide levels

Afghanistan? Afghanistan's valuable mineral resources, virtually untapped commercially, are estimated by geologists to be the world's largest and most valuable: at least US $1 trillion but more likely $3,000,000,000,000 ($3 trillion), which makes it the most valuable mining region on earth.[63] Iraq? Iraq's oil reserves back in 2010 were estimated officially at 143 billion barrels, making it the 3rd largest oil reserve in the world, bigger than Saudi Arabia, bigger than Russia, and bigger than the United States. More recent estimates put Iraq in 1st place – i.e. the largest oil reserves in the entire world at over 150 billion barrels of proven reserves. How much would that be worth? In March 2014 world crude oil prices were just over US $100 per barrel, which would make Iraq's proven reserves worth over $15,000,000,000,000 ($15 trillion). Of course, it still makes no moral sense, but it now makes the usual patriarchal capitalist sense. I suppose if the US plays their cards right, they might just recover the $6 trillion they will have spent on the wars to gain control of these $18 trillion in untapped assets. The human costs? Patriarchal capitalists only pretend to care (really, why else would the US be so keen on negotiating with the Taliban,[64] who make the US' allies in Saudi Arabia look positively progressive – but then again, even the latter seem to endorse prostitution[65]).

So very many ways to abuse the earth

In the words of the Sea Shepherd Conservation Society's Scott West: "In many ways, I think we are past the point of no return, but I'm not going to stop fighting."[66] And there really is still much reason for hope, with all of non-human Gaia holding their figurative collective breaths to see what we humans do. The intricate system that is Gaia will certainly self-heal with or without us humans being any part of it, and it's pretty clear that planet earth is already beginning to experience Gaia's natural "immune system" engaging, but it will be far more traumatic for all of Gaia to heal without us than if we finally begin repairing and reversing the damage we've wrought, even at this late hour. If we fail to even truly try? That will be a universal tragedy, and the Goddess Herself will weep.

How bad is this mess humans at the hands of patriarchy have created for Gaia? It would not be wrong to view the extremes of the natural world which have been having such profound impacts on people on every continent in the past decade as responses of Gaia's immune system to human inflicted pain and suffering (but know that Gaia's "immune response" is not some kind of punishment, selective or otherwise, it is a survival response just as our own human immune systems exhibit). Let's call it for what it truly is: Gaia has been and is being raped, exploited, tortured, sold, and violated just as so very many women, children, and the marginalized among the human species are. Documenting all of this patriarchal destruction of Gaia is not the purpose of this book, but here are a few examples which alone should make all of us stand up and do something, and do it fast.

Climate devastation

Nowhere is the interconnectedness of humans with the rest of Gaia more obvious and acute in its devastation than in human impact on earth's climate. In perhaps the ultimate ironic feedback loop, the triple whammy of **human-caused global warming**, **sea level rise**, and **ocean acidification** probably spell the end for huge segments of the human population, the breakdown of current human society, and the curtain call for the power structures and institutions we've been living under (so yes, there is some good news here, but this is not at all the way we want to get there). This book is intended neither to be a treatise nor even a primer on human-induced climate change, but these problems are so serious, so unequivocally caused by patriarchal power structures, and need so urgently to be addressed, I have to raise them in some detail. I've included multiple references to the scientific literature as well as popular sources and the press. I earnestly ask you to use these references as a launching point to educate yourself as much as you can about this most dire situation in which we humans have placed Gaia.

Global warming is real and the human cause of global warming is just as real. If you disagree, I'm sorry, you are being delusional. Imagine you have children, and even a few grandchildren. You find yourself not feeling very well at all. You go to your physician and she tells you the bad news: you have cancer, and it is very serious, perhaps terminal. You don't trust doctors, so you go to 99 more for a diagnosis. All but 3 of them give you the same dreaded result. If you went to 100 doctors to be tested for cancer, and 97 of them said you had a serious case of the disease, would you believe them? And if this were the case, wouldn't you do something for your children and grandchildren, even if it was perhaps too late to do anything for yourself? Only a sociopath would do nothing. Over 97% of climate scientists over the past 20 years concur that humans are causing global warming, and the resulting rises in sea level and in ocean acidification.[67] Human-caused global warming is exactly like the hypothetical cancer diagnosis, and for humanity and all of Gaia, it is just as serious, but all too real.

Humans cause global warming by emitting greenhouse gases from their industry, agriculture, fossil fuel production, much energy generation, and most of their modes of transportation. These greenhouse gases - primarily carbon dioxide (CO_2), methane (CH_4), nitrous oxide (N_2O), and fluorinated (F) gases – are called that because like the windows of a greenhouse they allow the atmosphere to be heated but do not allow as much heat to be dissipated as the earth's atmosphere absorbs. Among greenhouse gases, nitrous oxide and the fluorinated gases have by far "the greatest impact pound-for-pound on semi-permanent warming the atmosphere", but carbon dioxide and methane account for the largest quantities of emissions (in 2011, 84% and 9%, respectively) and are thus the major culprits in global warming.[68] While greenhouse gases are also produced by natural sources, humans are responsible for much of the release of these gases, directly by burning and through the decay of biomass from deforestation and land clearing, or indirectly via traditional rice production, cattle farming,[69] or thawing of permafrost due to human-induced global warming.[70,71] These last three sources are particularly serious due to the release of methane gas which has 21 times the effect of carbon dioxide on global warming. Carbon dioxide on the other hand accounts for 77% of greenhouse gases released worldwide, so while its inherent impact on global warming is the least among the greenhouse gases, it has the greatest impact due to its ubiquity.[72]

The production and use of fossil fuels is the single largest source of atmospheric CO_2: in the three decades between 1981 and 2011, CO_2 emissions from energy consumption and production accounted for about 75% of worldwide carbon dioxide emissions. What's worse, CO_2 emissions increased by an astounding 79% in this 30 year period, and just in the last decade, CO_2 emitted through energy consumption has increased by 34.4% - more than one-third. Who are the world's biggest CO_2 polluters? In 2011, China and the United States, accounting for 24% of the earth's human population threw a massive 44% of the total release of CO_2 into our atmosphere (27% and 17%[‡],

respectively[*]): more than *six times* the 7% of CO_2 released by all

of Africa, South America, and Central America combined (who

together comprise 22% of the earth's population). Among major

CO_2 emitters, the United States is by far the world's biggest

villain on a per capita basis, releasing 375% of the world average

of carbon dioxide per person (China releases 139% of the world

per capita average). Despite having only 4.5% of the world's

population, the United States is by far the absolute leader in

petroleum consumption, gulping down 21% - over 1/5th - of the

world's petroleum, 465% of the world per capita average

(meaning the average American consumes 4.65 times as much

petroleum as the average human), followed by China consuming

12% of petroleum annually (but only 60% of the world's average

per person).[73] Does this mean that for anything to seriously begin

to repair human damage to climate, the United States and China

above all must radically correct their energy consumption and

usage behavior? It most certainly does.

What does the on-going climate disaster mean for the

world's human population? Upwards of 2 billion people

(2,000,000,000) face starvation due to food shortages resulting

from global warming as soon as the year 2050,[74] and an

[‡] There is strong evidence China is underreporting its CO_2 output and energy consumption by 20% or more. The "real" number for China is probably closer to 23% of the world total, which would make the United States and China responsible for 50% of the world's CO_2 emissions (*The Economist*, 23 June 2012, "Warmed-up numbers: China may be severely underreporting its carbon emissions").

[*] Russia (5%), India (5%) and Japan (4%) round out the top 5

additional half a billion (500,000,000) face relocation from coastal areas by 2100.[75] About 1 billion face starvation due to the terrestrial affects of human-induced global warming (for example extremes of drought and rainfall and changing climate zones), and the other half due to the affects of ocean acidification.[76] Groundwater resources are *already* stressed for 1.7 billion of the world's people – 1/4th of the earth's human population – and this will only worsen as these stressed areas become increasingly arid throughout this century. The problems are particularly acute in the key agricultural region of the Central United States and the high-density population areas of China,[77] the same areas which are forecast to suffer the greatest effect of increased aridity due to human-induced global warming. In the Arctic, many "tipping points" may have already been reached, plunging that region into the realm of "dangerous climate change".[78] Ocean acidification threatens the very existence of life – all life – in the earth's oceans. It is very likely that much of our oceans will be dead, devoid of life, as soon as the middle of this century, with the Northern Pacific, Bering Sea, and Arctic Ocean areas particularly devastated. The world's oceans absorb 25% of the CO_2 emitted by humans every year, turning the oceans increasingly acidic in direct correlation with the increases in atmospheric CO_2.[79] This increased ocean acidification makes it impossible for the tiny marine creatures and corals at the base of the pelagic food chain to reproduce, because the shells of these creatures are literally dissolved by the acidic seawater before they reach maturity.[80] Ocean acidification thus poses an imminent threat to the survival of over 1,000,000,000 (1 billion) of the earth's people who rely on the oceans for their sustenance. Increases in ocean acidification are directly caused by human emissions of carbon dioxide into the atmosphere, further amplified by the loss of sea ice and glacial and ice sheet melting (also caused by human-induced global warming), all resulting in a rate of increase in ocean acidity 50 times higher than anything observed in our planet's history. The rate of increased ocean acidity is so high that by the end of this century, acidity is projected to be at levels not seen in the past 21 million years. Scientists doubt if ocean life – any ocean life – could adapt quickly enough in this extremely brief timeframe, thus leading to extinction of almost all marine life.[81] On top of acidification, the affects of significant warming of the oceans' depths occurring below 700 meters is not yet well understood but has been substantial, especially during the last decade[§] (as well as acting as a "heat bank" for future release).[82]

The Pliocene era (between 3 and 5 million years ago) was the most recent period in history when the earth's atmospheric heat trapping ability was like it is today. Atmospheric CO_2 levels reached as much as 415 parts per million (ppm) during the Pliocene. In May 2013, CO_2 levels reached 400 ppm for the first time in human history. So, scientists take the Pliocene era as a

---

§   This also explains the supposed "missing warming" of the ocean surface touted by climate change deniers as supposed evidence of global warming having stopped in the past decade. In fact just as with the atmosphere there has been very significant warming of the oceans throughout the past 50 years, it is only that most ocean warming (so far) has occurred at depths below 700 meters.

model for what we are experiencing now, and what we can expect in the near future. What were things like back then? Global average temperatures were about 4°C (7.2°F) warmer than today, but were considerably higher in polar regions where they were 10°C (18°F) warmer.[83] Current scientific models project our earth's temperatures will reach these very levels and patterns by the end of this century.[84] So other than being warmer, what were things like back in the Pliocene?

Sea levels ranged between 5 and 40 meters (16 to 131 feet) higher than today.[85] There is every indication that the lower end (+5 meters) of this range of increase will be reached by the year 2100, with sea levels continuing to rise for hundreds of years after that (sea level significantly lags CO_2 levels due to the long time needed to melt ice and heat water).[86] No less a capitalist establishment than the World Bank warns "there is little evidence that the international community has seriously considered the impact of SLR [Sea Level Rise]" and conclude it is necessary that "immediate planning for adaptation" commence. The Bank warns that a 5 meter rise in sea level would displace 5.6% of the earth's population, i.e. approximately half-a-billion (500,000,000) people, with countries such as the Bahamas, Vietnam,and Egypt severely impacted (and wetlands devastated most of all). The belly of the capitalist beast would by no means escape: US cities like Boston would resemble their appearance three centuries ago (but with many additional Harbor Islands),[87] New York's hurricane Sandy would have proven itself only a taste of things to come,[88] and Miami and south Florida would be pretty much gone completely, save for a new archipelago[89]. If the Greenland ice sheet were to melt completely, and the Antarctic ice sheet to melt partially - events that are likely to occur by the end of the millennium, but possibly much sooner than that - we would indeed experience Pliocene sea level rises,[90] or worse (and virtually all coastal cities around the world will be distant memories). In the words of geologist Richard Norris at Scripps Institute of Oceanography: "I think it is likely that all these [Pliocene] ecosystem changes could recur ... our dumping of heat and CO_2 into the ocean is like making an investment in a pollution 'bank'..."[91] If you're still not sufficiently scared, or convinced we humans need to do something major and now to stanch global warming, consider this: current scientific models project CO_2 levels of nearly 1000 ppm by the *end of this century* if we keep doing what we've been doing[92] - a CO_2 level more than twice that of the Pliocene, resulting in an earth unrecognizable if not simply uninhabitable. The World Bank could not have summed up the *current* situation any better: "these results are not speculative: the current concentration of GHG's [Green House Gases] is sufficient to drive global warming well into the next century, and much higher concentrations will undoubtedly be reached before any global agreement can be implemented."[93] Will the beautifully intricate system that is Gaia permit this to happen? No, she won't. But humans will no longer be part of the mix.

Extreme extremes

It is not completely correct to call all of what is happening to our atmosphere "climate change" – even the geology and day-to-day weather of the earth is being affected, with major human consequences. According to the US government's own assessment "the rising incidence of weather extremes will have increasingly negative impacts on crop and livestock productivity because critical thresholds are *already* being exceeded" [emphasis added]. There is growing evidence that warming in the Arctic (which is double the rest of the planet due to the impacts of atmospheric soot, tropospheric ozone, and methane from melting permafrost in addition to CO_2)[94] may well be driving the weather extremes being observed throughout the northern hemisphere due to a phenomenon known as "Arctic amplification" resulting in "stuck" weather systems, and hence areas of persistent severe drought or excessively wet conditions.[95] These extreme conditions are *already* occurring, and have been steadily worsening for the past half century. Planet-wide the trend has been for wet areas to get wetter, dry areas to get drier, and weather extremes to become increasingly extreme. Over the past 32 years, the number of natural catastrophes due to drought, flooding, extreme temperatures, and forest fires has increased worldwide by 350%. The 260% increase in natural catastrophes due to storms (e.g. hurricanes and tornadoes) during the same 1980-2012 period was only slightly lower.[96]

In the United States alone:

- the average precipitation in the Northeast region has increased 8% in the past decade, but the incidence of very heavy precipitation events in that region has risen 74%. Meanwhile, average precipitation has plummeted in Hawaii and portions of the Southwest by more than 15% in the same 10 year period.[97]

- in New England, since 1970 average annual temperatures have risen by 1.5°F overall, but 4°F in the winter. By the end of the century, Massachusetts climate will have "migrated" to conditions currently experienced in South Carolina.[98]

- The drought conditions persisting in the West over the past 10 years are the driest conditions that region has experienced in 800 years,[99] and it is only going to get significantly worse. In spring and early summer 2013, almost half of the western United States was locked in the region's worst drought in 60 years, resulting in a fire season that was two months longer and destroyed twice as much forest as was the average in the 1970s.[100] By the 2070s, precipitation in the critical spring and summer months in this region, together with the lower Midwest, Southwest, and South Central United States will have decreased by 20-30%, adding persistent severe drought in the nation's critical agricultural regions to fire conditions in Western forests. The drying will be even worse in the Pacific Northwest, which can expect more than 30% less precipitation during the warm (by then, hot) months of the year. Soil moisture throughout all of the US "breadbasket" and the Southwest is also projected to drop significantly (in many areas 15% or more) by the 2070s.[101]

- on top of drought, heat waves and extreme temperatures have already become commonplace in the United States and elsewhere, and that trend will unfortunately continue over the next decades and beyond. The spring and summer months of 2011 and 2012 both shattered records for the highest monthly average temperatures throughout the United States, with July 2012 the hottest month in that country's history. Heat waves by the 2070s will feature temperatures 10~15°F hotter than today's heat waves. Both the total number *and* intensity of tropical cyclones/hurricanes is expected to increase by 2100,[102] with the frequency of the most severe hurricanes (Category 4 and 5) increasing by 80% through 2080.[103]

The affects of human-caused global warming are not just confined to the United States, of course. The UK Met Office reported that the winter of 2013-14 was the wettest ever for England and Wales since at least 1766 (when record-keeping began); it was also the 5th warmest winter there (1.5 °C above average).[104] Climate change and global warming is not just having a pronounced affect on the more intuitively obvious weather and ocean conditions, but even on the earth's very geology. On 20 September 2002, the largest avalanche in modern times struck the village of Kani in the Caucasus mountains on the Russian/Georgian border. An entire glacier, bringing an enormous flow of boulders and mud along with it, slipped suddenly from the mountains high above, travelled 18 km at avalanche speeds, and destroyed the village, killing 120 of its 150 inhabitants.[105] The cause? Melting permafrost below the glacier. Of the one-third of the earth's surface covered in permafrost, a significant portion lies in mountain ranges, where it plays a crucial role acting as a kind of concrete holding the outer layers of these mountains in place. Ranges such as the Alps are particularly vulnerable, and in the past 20 years, permafrost in the Alps has become deeply thawed. The frequency of avalanches have been increasing greatly in the Alps over the past two decades, and it is just a matter of time before the next village or town in a mountain valley meets a similar fate to the village of Kani.[106] So yes, the willful negligence of humans toward earth's climate can actually bring down mountains.

Even more ways to kill Gaia

Great work, patriarchy! You designed plastic to last forever but made it disposable, transforming the five major ocean gyres into the five ocean garbage gyres, filled with mostly microscopic bits of plastic now found in *all* species of sea turtles, 44% of all seabirds, and 22% of cetaceans.[107] You've created a climate where the Western United States suffered its worst devastation from forest fires in history,[108] Europe is inundated with two "100 year floods" in only one decade,[109] and 10,000 people perished in flooding in India's earliest ever monsoon (one month too soon)[110] - and all of this just in the month of June 2013! Your terrestrial oil wells in the United States spill more oil every year than the Exxon Valdez tragedy,[111] you weaken faults and create earthquakes through your fracking processes (300 *per year* in the central and eastern United States in the last 3 years, compared with an annual average of only 21 per year before that),[112] and within a decade or so you may have poisoned virtually all of our water supply by injecting 30 *trillion* gallons of toxic waste (just in the United States) into deep underground wells which are now erupting into our drinking water. According to one former EPA engineering expert, "In 10 to 100 years we are going to find out that most of our groundwater is polluted. A lot of people are going to get sick, and a lot of people may die."[113] Consider sharks. These animals are portrayed as the embodiment of evil, when in fact they are essential to our ocean's food chain. The very survival of the ocean itself, which is the source of oxygen for one of every two breaths we take, depends on the survival of sharks. Human-caused shark deaths in 2012? Seven people died *worldwide* from shark attacks that year, while an average of 85 people *per day* in the United States were shot dead by guns.[114] Meanwhile, nearly 200,000,000 sharks are killed every year – over 500,000 *per day*, or 6 sharks *every second*. Lacking natural predators, sharks have survived on earth for at least 400 million years, but are likely to become extinct within decades due to human predation that knows no limit. Even worse, most sharks perish for their fins, the remainder of their body discarded as waste. A single bowl of shark fin soup – one of the ultimate patriarchal status symbols in China and other parts of the Far East - sells for €100. This bowl of wanton destruction and utter waste is also utterly tasteless and devoid of nutrition,[115,116]and yet the patriarchal appetite is never sated. If sharks are wiped out, the oceans will die, and if the oceans die, we die, too.

Patriarchy, you're through. Never come back.

Are there disturbing parallels between the devastation of the earth and the oppression of humans? Aren't there singular similarities between Gaia's assailants and the commonalty's tyrants? Of course there are: they are the same actors, their actions equally deliberate. Who are these perpetrators wantonly destroying Gaia? Who are these "humans" raping the rest of us with impunity? Patriarchy, of course.

It leaves you dumbfounded, doesn't it. Just in the few late 20th century genocides I've reviewed in this book, (and sadly this isn't even a comprehensive list), 11,000,000 people were brutally murdered, most often by the very ruling powers that should have been there to protect them. The wealthy, economically powerful, mostly capitalist, so-called highly developed nations stood by in each and every case and did absolutely *nothing*, even while having full knowledge of what was happening early in the devastation if not beforehand. Why? It is as if the unspeakable devastation was not just allowed, but encouraged. Wasn't it, patriarchy?

The exploitation, rape, selling and wanton destruction of the earth's creatures and resources that make up the rest of Gaia goes hand-in-hand with the patriarchy's exploitation, rape, selling and wanton destruction of all of us who make up the human Feminine, doesn't it? We must stop being afraid to know this, and state this openly and loudly as the fact it is. There is a war on women, a war on children, a war on the marginalized, a war on all of us who nurture and love, a war on Gaia. The attack on the Feminine and the attack on Gaia are both direct attacks on Goddess Herself. After they've finished with Gaia, the patriarchy are hell bent on discarding Her just as they discard so many women and children and innocents and wildlife and natural resources which they no longer find useful for their greedy enrichment or simply not suiting their fancy.

Patriarchy is like an accretion disk around a black hole, indiscriminately tearing apart all that come within its influence with no apparent hope of escape. But unlike a black hole, with patriarchy there really is a chance of escape, a certainty of escape even, you just have to know how to connect with and use what is already there and available to you, and understand the incredible synergies that develop when you begin using what is already the essential part of who you are.

Patriarchy, the speed and force of your devastating destructive power seems endless, and endlessly evil. But we aim to stop you, and we will. You've proven we cannot halt you using the methods you use or the structures you've put in place, despite truly heroic efforts by so many of us over the past 100 years and more in the women's and children's rights, feminist, anti-capitalist, and environmental movements. Our progress has been far too slow, too often our successes have been far too small, and the setbacks you construct are far too devastating. You are superb at playing your game, because of course you invented the game, you wrote the rules of the game, and you run the game. We "can't beat you at your own game", to use the American idiom, and we need to stop trying. We need to feel, think, and be outside of your patriarchal game, and we shall not play by any of your rules to do this. As individual parts of the Feminine, and as the vastly interconnected Feminine collective, we neither accept your suppositions nor your conclusions. We neither need nor want the gods you've constructed or the toxic religions that go along with them. The Feminine is intimately and infinitely interconnected, and limitlessly powerful, but feminine power bears no resemblance to the patriarchal kind. Our power comes from our deepest feelings, is implemented using our innermost intuitions, and all that we are and all that we do is based on love, not any bogus religious notion of love, but the love that interconnects all of us. So, patriarchy, you are warned – warned to be ready for the most loving, embracing, peaceful, and powerful revolution imaginable: the revolution of the Feminine. It has *not* been nice knowing you, patriarchy, and we are not the least bit sad to see you go.

"Why fight the 'natural' ... order of things?
Why? Because of this:—
one fine day, a purely predatory world
shall consume itself...
In an individual, selfishness uglifies the soul;
for the human species, selfishness is extinction."
                                           – David Mitchell, *Cloud Atlas*[117]

Chapter 1 - References

1 World Wildlife Fund, "How many species are we losing?," accessed 6 July 2013 from http://wwf.panda.org/about_our_earth/biodiversity/biodiversity/

2 bell hooks, "Understanding Patriarchy," p.1, Louisville Anarchist Federation (monograph)

3 Public Papers of the Presidents, "Military-Industrial Complex Speech, Dwight D. Eisenhower, 1961," accessed on 8 July 2013 from http://coursesa.matrix.msu.edu/~hst306/documents/indust.html

4 Center for Responsive Politics, 2012 Presidential Race, accessed 9 July 2013 from http://www.opensecrets.org/pres12/sectorall.php

5 Seth Cline, "12 Biggest Donors of the 2012 Elections," *US News & World Report (26 October 2012)*, accessed 9 July 2013 from http://www.usnews.com/news/articles/2012/10/26/12-biggest-donors-of-the-2012-election

6 Center for Responsive Politics

7 Credit Suisse Global Wealth Databook 2011, "The global wealth pyramid," accessed 8 July 2013 from http://anticap.wordpress.com/2011/10/20/the-global-wealth-pyramid/

8 Tyler Falk, "The global super-rich are even more wealthy than you can imagine," (20 June 2013), accessed 6 July 2013 from http://www.smartplanet.com/blog/bulletin/the-global-super-rich-are-even-more-wealthy-than-you-can-imagine/22385

9 Wearden, Graeme. "Oxfam: 85 Richest People as Wealthy as Poorest Half of the World." *Theguardian.com*. Guardian News and Media, 20 Jan. 2014. Web. 04 Mar. 2014.

10 T. Achtnich und H. Michel, "Geld Regiert die Welt", ARD, 13. January 2014, Dokumentarfilm, accessed on 14 June 2014 from http://www.ardmediathek.de/tv/Reportage-Dokumentation/Die-Story-im-Ersten-Geld-regiert-die-We/Das-Erste/Video?documentId=19067010&bcastId=799280

11 The Wall Street Journal, "BlackRock Reports First Quarter 2014 Diluted EPS of $4.40, or $4.43 as adjusted", 17 April 2014, accessed on 14 June 2014 from http://online.wsj.com/article/PR-CO-20140417-905435.html

12 Tax Justice Network, "Blog Steuergerechtigkeit," 23 January 2013, accessed 6 July 2013 from http://steuergerechtigkeit.blogspot.de/2013/01/neue-erkenntnisse-zu-den-kosten-des.html

13 Eurostat, "Unemployment rates, seasonally adjusted, May 2013.png," European Union (May 2013), accessed 6 July 2013 from http://epp.eurostat.ec.europa.eu/statistics_explained/index.php?title=File:Unemployment_rates,_seasonally_adjusted,_May_2013.png&file timestamp=20130702091731

14 Eurostat, "File:Youth unemployment, 2012Q4 (%).png," European Union, accessed 6 July 2014 from http://epp.eurostat.ec.europa.eu/statistics_explained/index.php?title=File:Youth_unemployment,_2012Q4_%28%25%29.png&filetimestamp=20130418091546

15 Citizens for Tax Justice, "Apple is Not Alone" (2 June 2013) accessed 6 July 2013 from http://ctj.org/ctjreports/2013/06/apple_is_not_alone.php#.Ucov3usrV1O

16 Marc Pitzke, "Offshore-Leaks: Gigantisches Netzwerk der Steuerhinterzieher enthüllt," *Spiegel Online (04. April 2013)*, accessed 9 July 2013 from http://www.spiegel.de/wirtschaft/soziales/offshore-leaks-gigantisches-netzwerk-der-steuerhinterzieher-enthuellt-a-892406.html

17 Économie, " 'Offshore Leaks': les détails du projet," *Le Monde (04. Avril 2013)*, accessed 9 July 2013 from http://www.lemonde.fr/economie/article/2013/04/04/offshore-leaks-les-details-du-projet_3153470_3234.html

18 Freedom on Film, University of Georgia, 'Black and Women in Augusta Golf," accessed 8 July 2013 from http://www.civilrights.uga.edu/cities/augusta/golf_tournaments.htm

19 Wealthx.com "The World Ultra Wealth Report 2012-2013," accessed 8 July 2013 from wealthx.com/wealthreport

20 World Bank, "World Development Indicators database" downloaded 1 July 2013 from http://databank.worldbank.org/data/download/GDP.pdf

21 Inter-Parliamentary Union, "Women in national parliaments: Situation as of 1st June 2013," accessed 1 July 2013 from http://www.ipu.org/wmn-e/classif.htm

22 Maps of World, "Women Workforce Map," accessed 6 July 2013 from http://www.mapsofworld.com/thematic-maps/world-women-in-workforce-map.htm

23 Catalyst, "No News Is Bad News: Women's Leadership Still Stalled in Corporate America," accessed 6 July 2013 from http://www.catalyst.org/media/no-news-bad-news-womens-leadership-still-stalled-corporate-america

24 Frauen-lohnspiegel.de, "Noch vielfältige Nachteile für Frauen im Erwerbsleben," (2013), accessed 10 July 2013 from http://www.lohnspiegel.de/main/lohnspiegel-spezial/frauenlohnspiegel/frauengehalter-niedriger

25 Simon Rogers, "International women's day: the pay gap between men and women for your job," *The Guardian (8 March 2011)*, accessed 6 July 2013 from http://www.guardian.co.uk/news/datablog/2011/mar/08/international-womens-day-pay-gap

26 MSN News, "50 years after Equal Pay Act's passage, gender wage gap still persists," web posted 13 June 2013, accessed 6 July 2013 from http://news.msn.com/us/50-years-after-equal-pay-acts-passage-gender-wage-gap-still-persists

27 ARD (Sendung), "Die Sexismus-Debatte: Was hat sie gebracht?," *Menschen bei Maischberger (16. April 2013)*, accessed 10 July 2013 from http://www.daserste.de/unterhaltung/talk/menschen-bei-maischberger/sendung/16042013-sexismus-debatte-100.html

28 National Committee on Pay Equity, "The Wage Gap, by Gender and Race," as reported by Infoplease.com, accessed on 10 July 2013 from

http://www.infoplease.com/ipa/A0882775.html

29 U.S. Census Bureau, Statistical Abstract of the United States (2012) p. 840, accessed on 10 July 2013 from http://www.census.gov/compendia/statab/2012/tables/12s1337.pdf

30 U.S. Census Bureau

31 Data Blog, "Single fathers: UK statistics," *The Guardian (13 June 2013)* accessed 10 July 2013 from http://www.guardian.co.uk/news/datablog/2013/jun/13/single-fathers-uk-statistics

32 Astrid Joosten, "Alleinerziehende - von der Gesellschaft im Stich gelassen," *Brigitte.de* (2013), accessed 10 July 2013 from http://www.brigitte.de/frauen/gesellschaft/dossier-alleinerziehend-565687/

33 Rick Mathews, "27.3% of Single Parent Households Live in Poverty" (2012), accessed 6 July 2013 from http://www.policymic.com/articles/11316/27-3-of-single-parent-households-live-in-poverty

34 Jaqueline Kirby, "Single-parent Families in Poverty," accessed 6 July 2013 from http://www3.uakron.edu/schulze/401/readings/singleparfam.htm

35 Joosten

36 "ILO: Milliardenprofite aus moderner Sklaverei", *Neues Deutschland* (20. Mai 2014), accessed 24 May 2014 from http://www.neues-deutschland.de/artikel/933515.ilo-milliardenprofite-aus-moderner-sklaverei.html

37 World Health Organization, "Global and regional estimates of violence against women," (2013), accessed 10 July 2013 from http://apps.who.int/iris/bitstream/10665/85239/1/9789241564625_eng.pdf

38 Ami Sedghi, "Women and the criminal justice system: what do the latest statistics show?," *The Guardian (22 November 2012)* accessed 6 July 2013 from http://www.guardian.co.uk/news/datablog/2012/nov/22/women-criminal-justice-system-statistics-representation

39 AL Kellermann, JA Mercy, "Men, women, and murder: gender-specific differences in rates of fatal violence and victimization," *J Trauma 1992 Jul;33(1):1-5*, accessed 6 July 2013 from http://www.ncbi.nlm.nih.gov/pubmed/1635092

40 Bureau of Justice Statistics, US Department of Justice, accessed 6 July 2013 from http://www.bjs.gov/

41 BBC News, "Rape affects almost 20% of US women, study says," BBC News US & Canada (15 December 2011), accessed 6 July 2013 from http://www.bbc.co.uk/news/world-us-canada-16192494

42 Rape, Abuse & Incest National Network (RAINN), "Statistics," accessed 9 July 2013 from http://www.rainn.org/statistics

43 SURF Survivors Fund

44 Fabiola Ortiz, "Rape in Brazil Still an Invisible Crime," *Inter Press Service News Agency (24 June 2013)*, accessed 10 July 2013 from http://www.ipsnews.net/2013/06/rape-in-brazil-still-an-invisible-crime/

45 Patrick Kingsley, "80 sexual assaults in one day – the other story of Tahrir

Square," *The Guardian (5 July 2013)*,
http://www.guardian.co.uk/world/2013/jul/05/egypt-women-rape-sexual-assault-tahrir-square

46 Ashfaq Yusufzai, "Acid Survivors Say Theirs Is a Fate Worse Than Death," Inter Press Service News Agency (28 June 2013), accessed 10 July 2013 from http://www.ipsnews.net/2013/06/acid-survivors-say-theirs-is-a-fate-worse-than-death/

47 Cordula Meyer, Conny Neumann, Fidelius Schmid et al., "Ungeschützt," *Der Spiegel 22/2013* (27. Mai 2013), S. 56-65

48 Nicola Albrecht, Heiko Käberich, Daniel Strobel, "Frauenhandel in China," ml Mona Lisa, ZDF (20 April 2013)

49 Nicola Albrecht, Liu Jia, Heiko Käberich, "Entführt und Verkauft," Auslands Journal, ZDF Studio Peking (29 Aug 2012)

50 Amy Hudnall, Appalachian State University, "Conflict and Peace" (2010), accessed 5 July 2013 from http://firstyearseminar.appstate.edu/conflict-and-peaceunderstanding-genocide-20th-century

51 The Cambodian Genocide Program, Yale University (2010), accessed 5 July 2013 from http://www.yale.edu/cgp/

52 Samantha Power, "A Problem from Hell: America and the Age of Genocide," C-SPAN interview 16 June 2002, accessed 5 July 2013 from http://www.booknotes.org/Watch/170542-1/Samantha+Power.aspx

53 SURF Survivors Fund, "Statistics of the Rwandan Genocide," accessed 5 July 2013 from http://survivors-fund.org.uk/resources/rwandan-history/statistics/

54 Rory Carroll, "US chose to ignore Rwandan genocide," *The Guardian (31 March 2004)*, accessed 5 July 2013 from http://www.guardian.co.uk/world/2004/mar/31/usa.rwanda

55 United to End Genocide, 'DR Congo,' accessed 5 July 2013 from http://endgenocide.org/conflict-areas/dr-congo/

56 United to End Genocide, 'Sudan', accessed 5 July 2013 http://endgenocide.org/conflict-areas/sudan/

57 Watson Institute for International Studies, "Costs of War: Iraq 10 Years After Invasion," Brown University, accessed on 5 July 2013 from http://costsofwar.org/iraq-10-years-after-invasion

58 Watson Institute for International Studies, "Costs of War: Iraq 10 Years After Invasion, Direct War Deaths," Brown University, accessed 5 July 2013 from http://costsofwar.org/sites/all/themes/costsofwar/images/Direct-War-Deaths%282%29.pdf

59 Iraq Analysis Group, "The Rising Costs of the Iraq War," (21 March 2007), accessed 5 July 2013 from http://www.iraqanalysis.org/publications/235

60 Bill van Auken, "The Most Expensive War in World History: Costs of Iraq, Afghanistan wars could rise to $6 trillion,"
Centre for Research on Globalization (2 April 2013), accessed on 5 July 2013 from http://www.globalresearch.ca/the-most-expensive-war-in-world-history-costs-of-iraq-afghanistan-wars-could-rise-to-6-

trillion/5329432

61 Edward Wong, "Hussein Charged with Genocide in 50,000 Deaths," *New York Times (April 5, 2006)*, accessed 5 July 2013 from http://www.nytimes.com/2006/04/05/world/middleeast/05iraq.html? pagewanted=all

62 Hassan Hafidh, "China CPPE, SCOP Secure $317 Million Iraq Oil Pipeline Contract," *The Wall Street Journal (2 July 2013)*, accessed on 5 July 2013 from http://online.wsj.com/article/BT-CO-20130702-708976.html

63 Kim Sengupta, "Afghanistan's resources could make it the richest mining region on earth," *The Independent (UK) (15 June 2010)* accessed 5 July 2013 from http://www.independent.co.uk/news/world/asia/afghanistans-resources-could-make-it-the-richest-mining-region-on-earth-2000507.html

64 Dion Nissenbaum, "Taliban's Sign Scuttles Negotiation Plans," *The Wall Street Journal (3 July 2013)*, accessed 5 July 2013 from http://online.wsj.com/article/SB10001424127887323899704578584521481012596.html

65 Leon Marino, "Legalized Prostitution in Salafi Wahabi Sect Society," (13 June 2012), accessed 5 July 2013 from http://sunnitigerscamp.blogspot.com/2012/06/legalized-prostitution-in-salafi-wahabi.html

66 Scott West, former US Environmental Protection Agency agent, currently Sea Shepherd's Director of Intelligence and Investigations, accessed 17 May 2013, http://www.eenews.net/stories/1059981212

67 John Cook, Dana Nuccitelli, Sarah A. Green et al., "Quantifying the consensus on anthropogenic global warming in the scientific literature," *Environ. Res. Lett. 8* (2013), doi: http://dx.doi.org/10.1088/1748-9326/8/2/024024. This study reviewed almost 12,000 scientific papers published about climate change in the past 20 years and found that virtually all – over 97% - agree that we are experiencing major human-caused global warming. In the authors' words "the number of papers rejecting the consensus on AGW [Anthropogenic Global Warming, i.e. human-induced global warming] is a vanishingly small proportion of the published research."

68 United States Environmental Protection Agency (US EPA), Sources of Greenhouse Gas Emissions, accessed 2 July 2013, http://www.epa.gov/climatechange/ghgemissions/sources.html

69 Angela R. Moss, Jean-Pierre Jouany and John Newbold, "Methane Production by ruminants: its contribution to global warming," *Ann. Zootech. 49* (2000) 231–253, http://www.bashaar.org.il/files/125122005103109.pdf. As of a decade ago, 12% more methane (CH_4) was released to the atmosphere annually than could be taken up by natural methane 'sinks.' The major sources of CH_4 are enteric fermentation (animal guts) and animal waste (43%), paddy rice production (41%), and biomass burning (16%). N.B. this does not include CH_4 release from permafrost (see Buis and

Jarrell).
70 Alan Buis, "Is a Sleeping Climate Giant Stirring in the Arctic," NASA Jet
Propulsion Laboratory, (10 June 2013), accessed 2 July 2013,
http://www.nasa.gov/topics/earth/features/earth20130610.html#.UdM5Hl
MrV69.
Permafrost covers over 25% of the northern hemisphere's exposed land
area. Unfortunately, current climate models do not adequately account for
release of CO_2 and CH_4 from thaw of the permafrost. Quantifying the
release of carbon-gases from permafrost thaw is an intense area of current
research.
71 Samantha Jarrell, "A thawing, rotting Arctic?," National Snow & Ice Data
Center *Icelights* (3 May 2013), accessed 2 July 2013
http://nsidc.org/icelights/2013/05/03/a-thawing-rotting-arctic/
72 US EPA
73 U.S. Energy Information Administration. Accessed 30 June 2013.
http://www.eia.gov/countries/
74 John Vidal, "Millions face starvation as world warms," *The Observer* (13
April 2013), accessed 21 April 2013, http://www.guardian.co.uk/global-
development/2013/apr/13/climate-change-millions-starvation-scientists
75 Susmita Dasgupta, Benoit Laplante, Craig Meisner et al., "The Impact of
Sea Level Rise on Developing Countries: A Comparative Analysis," World
Bank Policy Research Working Paper 4136 (WPS4136), February 2007
76 National Climate Assessment (Draft) v.11 (2013), United Sates National
Climate Assessment and Development Advisory Committee, accessed 30
June 2013, http://ncadac.globalchange.gov/download/NCAJan11-2013-
publicreviewdraft-fulldraft.pdf
77 Tom Gleeson, Yoshihide Wada, Marc F. P. Bierkens and Ludovicus P. H.
van Beek, "Water balance of global aquifers revealed by groundwater
footprint," *Nature 488, 197-200 (9 August 2012)*, doi:10.1038/nature11295
78 CSIC, Consejo Superior de Investigaciones Científicas (30 January 2012).
"Arctic is already suffering the effects of a dangerous climate change."
ScienceDaily. Accessed 1 July 2013, from http://www.sciencedaily.com
/releases/2012/01/120130171913.htm
79 National Climate Assessment, p. 89
80 Arctic Monitoring and Assessment Program (2013), "Arctic Ocean
Acidification Assessment: Summary for Policymakers," accessed 1 July
2013, http://www.amap.no/documents/doc/AMAP-Arctic-Ocean-
Acidification-Assessment-Summary-for-Policy-makers/808
81 National Climate Assessment pp. 69 - 70
82 Magdalena A. Balmaseda, Kevin E. Trenberth and Erland Källén,
"Distinctive climate signals in reanalysis of global ocean heat content,"
Geophysical Research Letters 40(9) (16 May 2013), pp. 1754-1759, DOI:
10.1002/grl.50382
83 Robert Monroe, "What does 400 ppm look like?," *The Keeling Curve* (25
April 2013), Scripps Institution of Oceanography, accessed 1 July 2013,
from keelingcurve.ucsd.edu/what-does-400-ppm-look-like

84 National Climate Assessment

85 Monroe

86 National Climate Assessment

87 Union of Concerned Scientists, *Confronting Climate Change in the US Northeast: Massachusetts*, accessed from http://www.cityofboston.gov/Images_Documents/MA%20confronting %20climate%20change%20in%20US%20Northeast_tcm3-19616.pdf

88 New York City Panel on Climate Change, *Climate Risk Information 2013: Observations, Climate Change Projections, and Maps* (June 2013), accessed 2 July 2013 from http://www.nyc.gov/html/planyc2030/downloads/pdf/npcc_climate_risk_in formation_2013_report.pdf

89 Jeff Goodell, "Goodbye, Miami," *Rolling Stone*, 20 June 2013, accessed 2 July 2013, http://www.rollingstone.com/politics/news/why-the-city-of-miami-is-doomed-to-drown-20130620

90 Jonathan T. Overpeck, Bette L. Otto-Bliesner, Gifford H. Miller et al., "Paleocentric Evidence for Future Ice-Sheet Instability and Rapid Sea-Level Rise," *Science*, Vol 311, 24 March 2006, pp 1747-1750

91 Monroe

92 Intergovernmental Panel on Climate Change, "Carbon Dioxide: Projected Emissions and Concentrations," accessed 2 July 2013 from http://www.ipcc-data.org/observ/ddc_co2.html

93 World Bank p. 45

94 Arctic Monitoring and Assessment Program (AMAP), "Short-lived Climate Forcers Affecting the Arctic," September 2009, accessed 3 July 2013 from http://www.amap.no/documents/doc/short-lived-climate-forcers-affecting-the-arctic/11

95 Jennifer Francis, "Linking Weird Weather to Rapid Warming of the Arctic." *Environment 360* (5 March 2012) Accessed 1 July 2013, from http://e360.yale.edu/feature/linking_weird_weather_to_rapid_warming_of _the_arctic/2501/

96 Münchener Rückversicherungs-Gesellschaft, "Natural Catastrophies 2012" (January 2013) accessed 3 July 2013 from http://www.munichre.com/app_pages/www/@res/pdf/media_relations/pres s_releases/2013/natural-catastrophes-2012-wold-map_en.pdf

97 National Climate Assessment pp. 20 - 30

98 Union of Concerned Scientists

99 National Climate Assessment, pp. 51 - 52

100 James West, "How Climate Change Makes Wildfires Worse," *Mother Jones* (13 June 2013), accessed 3 July 2013 from http://www.motherjones.com/environment/2013/06/climate-change-making-wildfires-worse

101 National Climate Assessment p. 44, 58

102 Kerry A. Emmanuel, "Downscaling CMIP5 climate models shows increased tropical cyclone activity over the 21st century," Proceedings of the National Academy of Sciences, (8 July 2013), doi:

10.1073/pnas.1301293110, accessed 11 July 2013 from http://www.pnas.org/content/early/2013/07/05/1301293110.abstract

103 National Climate Assessment, pp. 52 – 54, 62

104 UK Met Office, "Wettest winter for England and Wales since 1766," (27 February 2014), accessed 5 March 2014 from http://www.metoffice.gov.uk/news/releases/archive/2014/early-winter-stats

105 Wilfried Haeberli (Interview) *Horizonte 30. September 2012,* SRF, http://www.srf.ch/player/tv/horizonte/video/interview-mit-wilfried-haeberli-geowissenschaftler-uni-zuerich?id=cd474fce-655e-4b68-af31-d95487518ffd

106 Christian H. Schulz, "Gefahr aus den Bergen" (Film) (2011), ZDF, accessed 3 July 2013 from http://www.zdf.de/ZDFmediathek/beitrag/video/1077642/#/beitrag/video/1077642/Gefahr-aus-den-Bergen

107 5 Gyres Institute, "What is the Problem?," (2013), accessed 11 July 2013 from http://5gyres.org/what_is_the_issue/the_problem/

108 InfoPlease.com, accessed 11 July 2013 from http://www.infoplease.com/ipa/A0778688.html

109 Günther Jauch, "Jahrhundertflut, die Zweite – haben wir denn nichts gelernt", (9. Juni 2013), accessed 11 July 2013 from http://daserste.ndr.de/guentherjauch/rueckblick/hochwasser1611.html

110 UPI, "Indian lawmaker says flooding death toll could reach 10,000," (30 June 2013), accessed 11 July 2013 from http://www.upi.com/Top_News/World-News/2013/06/30/Indian-lawmaker-says-flooding-death-toll-could-reach-10000/UPI-56691372567186/#ixzz2YljtDsps

111 Mike Soraghan, "U.S. well sites in 2012 discharged more than Valdez," Energy Wire (8 July 2013), accessed 11 July 2013 from http://www.eenews.net/stories/1059983941

112 William L. Ellsworth, "Injection-Induced Earthquakes," *Science Vol. 341 no. 6142 (12 July 2013),* DOI: 10.1126/science.1225942, accessed 11 July 2013 from http://www.sciencemag.org/content/341/6142/1225942

113 Abraham Lustgarten and ProPublica, "Are Fracking Wastewater Wells Poisoning the Ground beneath Our Feet?," *Scientific American (21 June 2012),* accessed 11 July 2013 from http://www.scientificamerican.com/article.cfm?id=are-fracking-wastewater-wells-poisoning-ground-beneath-our-feeth

114 Christ Christof and Ilan Kolet, "American Gun Deaths to Exceed Traffic Fatalities by 2015," *Bloomberg.com* (19 December 2012), accessed 11 July 2013 from http://www.bloomberg.com/news/2012-12-19/american-gun-deaths-to-exceed-traffic-fatalities-by-2015.html

115 Simon Crerar, "Is China's shark-fin soup addiction driving sharks to extinction?," news.com.au (7 June 2013), accessed 11 July 2013 from http://www.news.com.au/travel/news/is-china8217s-sharkfin-soup-addiction-driving-sharks-to-extinction/story-e6frfq80-1226659462717

116 Judith Adlhoch, Markus Strober, und Hannes Jaenicke, "Im Einsatz für Haie," (2011), Dokumentarfilm

117 David Mitchell, *Cloud Atlas: A Novel*, Random House, 2012, Kindle Edition

Chapter 2

Love

The good people in the world will find each other,
and through their Love
they will bring about the change
that only Love brings

No matter how hard the patriarchal capitalists try to prevent it, no matter how hard the archons and their minion hierarchy try to prevent this from happening, the good people of the world will indeed find each other. The good people of the world will find each other because they will recognize each other. The recognition may be subtle and most often it will not be perfectly clear, but it will be a real recognition. You *always* find each other. Why? How do you recognize each other so that you find each other? Love, of course. Love is the space between matter, and also the space between anti-matter. Love is your true weapon against patriarchy, the archons, and anything or anyone who goes against Goddess. Of course, for Love to actually *be* Love, it must be active – there is no such thing as "passive Love", Love is never passive in any way.

Let's explore a bit more what Love is – more than just "where" it is (i.e. in the space between matter, and the space between anti-matter), although we really can only explore Love and not define it in 4D, for *Love can only be felt* with true feeling and never defined. You know Love when you feel it, and only when you feel it. (And that last sentence is really funny if you consider it: you cannot "know" what Love is, you can only *feel* Love – such are the inadequacies of human language in a patriarchal-dominated earth-plane). *Love is inter-dimensional* – and by inter-dimensional we mean Love is not just high dimensional (8D+), and obviously it is not just lower-dimensional (1D ~ 4D) or mid-dimensional (5D ~ 7D), but Love is truly *inter*-dimensional, embracing all of the dimensions, yes, absolutely all of them! Just think of Love in terms of Tantric Love – there is absolutely no upper limit on Love's dimensionality! As we said a little bit ago, *Love is active*. There is no possibility of Love being inactive; anything that might seem like Love but is inactive is in the realm of false yang/false yin, and is not in any way Love. Sadly there are people who to a lesser or greater extent think they can hold back their so-called love, or make their so-called love conditional. None of that is Love. Look no further than the Love of mothers for their children and you will know what it means that Love is always and only active. *Love is total, Love is unconditional.* Love completely encompasses true yin and true yang. That is to say, *true yin and true yang are properties of Love*, but they do not define Love. Nonetheless if one follows true yin and true yang, they are operating in the realm of Love, it can be no other way. How is it that Love seems to grow every moment? This is because *Love is limitless*. Nothing demonstrates this better than Tantra – every Tantric Love experience reaches new "heights" of dimensions, there is no limit! *Tantra embraces the infinite dimensionality of Love*. Love seems illogical in the same way that quantum logic seems illogical in a patriarchally-dominated earth-plane. Of course the universe **is** quantum, and not Newtonian; in just the same way, *Love is quantum*. How does one fall so deeply and "illogically" in Love? Because Love truly *is* quantum and obeys no rules of Newtonian logic. Can your Love be in two places simultaneously? Of course! Can Love jump from one dimension to an entirely (seemingly) distant dimension instantaneously without crossing the intervening dimensions? Absolutely! And Love cannot be contaminated, *Love is pure. Love unnerves the patriarchy and their system. Love embraces the Goddess-centric.* Is what you are doing upsetting capitalists and all manner of patriarchal types? If so, you are acting in Love, for sure! Does what you are doing make the Goddess-centric (regardless of how hard they may still be to find) smile warmly and embrace you, however bashfully? If so, you are loving! Again, *only Love can bring about the change that Love brings.* This may sound self-referential, and from any perspective of Newtonian logic, it indeed is, but from a Love perspective, from the point of view of quantum logic, this statement makes – that is, *feels* utter sense.

Expressing true feeling with words in 4D is a difficult and imperfect task, and expressing Love with 4D words is much more so, but I hope you can feel from what is written here even a little bit of what Love truly is. Truly, Love can only be felt.
There are other attributes we could use to try and describe Love, and even though attempting to describe Love in words is inadequate, here is a summary of the attributes of Love we've been describing:

- *Love can only be felt*
- *Love is inter-dimensional*
- *Love is active*
- *Love is total*
- *Love is unconditional*
- *true yin and true yang are properties of Love (but they do not define Love)*
- *Love is limitless*
- *Tantric Love embraces the infinite dimensionality of Love*
- *Love is quantum, and the logic of Love is quantum logic*
- *Love unnerves the patriarchy and their system*
- *Love is pure*
- *Love embraces the Goddess-centric*
- *only Love brings about the change that Love brings!*

Love's attributes are not at all theoretical, but indeed more real than most of what still passes for reality in these late days of the archono-patriarchal earth-plane. The archons cannot stop Love, no matter how much it bothers them. Their minions cannot stop Love, no matter how hard they try and even seemingly succeed in convincing others that Love is not what it is. *Love embraces Truth. Love is utterly tenacious*, it never surrenders, never gives up, no matter how dire things may appear, no matter how circumstances may be piled up against Love, no matter how deliberate Love may be under attack, Love does not give up, and Love is still utterly tenacious. How can Love be so strong in this regard? Because *Love embraces Truth, Truth seeks Love*. With Love there is always Truth, but even with Truth, Love may still be lacking. The "true-true" frequently referred to in the book and movie *Cloud Atlas*, the "true-true" being searched for by the characters in the story, is nothing less than Truth seeking Love, and ultimately Love embracing Truth. Truth without Love is still Truth, but Truth without Love has a melancholy emptiness. Truth without Love is true yang missing true yin. *Love is fulfilled true yin and true yang, neither lacking the other, Love is the very definition of fulfillment*. There are few people in the world who are truly *in Love* (and by "in Love" I mean in a *state* of Love, not necessarily in Love with someone else) but there are substantially more people who are *in Truth* and thus seeking Love, but who are not "in Love". For them, true yin is missing. But while this situation is kind of sad, it is also very encouraging, for these are exactly the large majority of people who are poised to fully embrace the Feminine, overthrow patriarchy, and restore the earth-plane to Goddess and Gaia, to a state of Love. It is necessary for someone to be "in Truth" for them to be "in Love", a kind of prerequisite. There are those who recognize Truth but choose to ignore it. These people can never be "in Love" because they aren't "in Truth". Sadly there are many who embrace the Truth but work so hard to try and acquire Love: these are the people who are really most ready to receive and understand and *act* on their true feelings. Never forget that without action, there is no Love. *Love is uncompromising* about this; well, Love is just uncompromising – in action, in Truth, in all of its aspects. Just think of the Sea Shepherd Conservation Society and their relationship with the whales, dolphins, and all creatures of the sea: there is no compromise in their Love, just as a mother for her child, or a lover for her beloved, Sea Shepherd does and will do anything in Love without compromise for our oceans.

How does Love "work"? *Love works multidimensionally in the space between matter (and anti-matter), and is the most fundamental manifestation of quantum entanglement* (which is now being openly demonstrated by the earth-plane scientific community on a macroscopic scale). This is why Love can act across any distance of space – or of time. This is why Love persists throughout the earth-plane's perceived past, present, and future.

And so here are a few more attributes of Love to add to our earlier list:

- *Love embraces Truth, Truth seeks Love*
- *Love is utterly tenacious*
- *Love is fulfilled true yin and true yang, neither lacking the other*
- *Love is the very definition of abundance*
- *Love is uncompromising*
- *Love works multidimensionally in the space between matter and anti-matter*
- *Quantum phenomena are manifestations of Love*

Love is Feminine

*Feminine Love **is** Love*

Goddess Liberated

Chapter 3

The Three Realms of Consciousness

Meet the Dyads

Let's go on a *Gedankenreise*, a thought-trip, to the two-dimensional world of the Dyads. On our *Gedankenreise*, imagine you are tasked to teach the three-dimensional concept of thickness (height/depth) in a two-dimensional world inhabited by two-dimensional beings, the Dyads. How will you explain a 3D concept like thickness to entities who only know a 2D world? You notice when looking down at the Dyads' world that in addition to the 2D Dyads who inhabit it, their world seems to be filled with squares scattered among otherwise empty space, but not just squares, there are two kinds of squares: hollow squares made up of line segments, and filled-in, solid ones. Whether they know it or not, thickness is the fundamental concept to understanding the Dyad universe. It turns out the filled-in squares are actually 3D cubic columns passing through the Dyads' 2D planar world, whereas the hollow squares really are just 2D hollow squares. These 3D columns are in fact the links that connect the Dyads' world to other Dyad worlds, and are the very structures that hold the Dyad universe together! But the Dyads don't know these other Dyad worlds exist, and can't easily tell there are two kinds of apparently square objects in their world; both types, hollow and filled-in, just seem to be squares. As you get to know the Dyads better and they begin to trust you, you learn there are a few Dyads who notice that not all squares are really the same; some squares make a thud when you bump into them, but others have a hollow ring. The real Dyad universe is 3D, yet the Dyads can only see and physically sense line segments in their 2D pseudo-reality. A few Dyads believe this is significant, and have even developed a concept they call "Squin/Squang" to teach other Dyads about the two kinds of squares. But even for the most highly developed among the Dyad sages, extending the concept of a filled-in square to one of 3D thickness is, and will always be, beyond their conscious ken. Unfortunately you also encounter the Darchons – sinister controlling thought-forms who are feared by many Dyads, and sadly worshipped by many Dyads for the same reason. These Darchons have convinced most Dyads that there is only one kind of object in their world, the 2D square, and *all* squares are the same. To enquire further is evil and blasphemous, all Dyads should just keep about their work, the Darchons will watch over them as benevolent overlords, uh, gods. Despite this, there are fortunately some Dyad sages, few in number but sincere in their seeking of the truth, who keep teaching the truth. And you learn that Dyads, when they are truly in touch with their feelings and their real innermost selves, can feel a concept that can only be described as 3D! Some of them even report dreaming in 3D, and during dreaming it makes perfect sense to them, yet when they awaken, it no longer makes any sense, and they find themselves once again in an apparently 2D world.

Now, suppose the hollow squares represent "mentality", the filled-in squares represent "physicality", and the 3D columns represent "feeling". Reread the Dyad story in this context. Can you sense the parallels to our own universe?

True Art

Artists are dancers, sculptors, photographers, musicians, writers and poets, but also athletes, cooks, shaman, mothers, and of course, lovers. Artists can be geologists working to preserve Gaia's structure from disease and disaster, biologists striving to save bees or cetaceans, farmers who practice sustainable agriculture, and all those who develop truly clean energy. There are myriad ways to be an artist, limitless ways you can execute your art, and all of them constitute Goddess – what could be more wonderful than that?! There are only two requirements for art to truly be art: it must connect true feeling with the physical world, and it must touch a being as true feeling, even if the only being it seems to touch is you, the artist. By "being" I don't just mean a person, but any of Gaia's diverse life forms, or even Gaia Herself. When you create art, there is a direct intuitive connection between what you truly feel and what the physical-you creates. In turn, your art creates a visceral reaction in whatever being receives your art. Your art is a gift of your true feeling to the universe. The visceral reaction that art produces cannot be tricked into mentality, and true art is always visceral (the visceral feeling of amazing sex is art of the highest order). The gift of your art is no trivial thing, either. Your art is a gift from you to the universe of a brand new creation. When we create art, we ourselves become in physicality the creator goddesses who we truly are in the realm of feeling.

You may analyze art from the box of mentality - the technique used to sculpt or paint it, the modes and chord progressions, the meter and rhythm of the verse, or even the meter and rhythm of sex – but none of these things "go through your head" when you are touched by art, do they? Indeed, nothing goes through your *head* at all! True art can neither be created nor experienced mentally. Real art is always experienced viscerally. It must be felt. It is only after their visceral response to art that people begin to "step it down" to the level of mentality. Consider purely literary art (and what makes it different from many other art forms). With the written word it is impossible *not* to traverse the space of mentality, due to its inherent use of the mental construct that is language. The written word is unavoidably executed in a Mental medium.[§] The written-word artist strives to make her work as intuitive and visceral as possible, but literary art cannot circumvent mentality to directly reach the recipient of the artwork. In contrast, nonverbal art - e.g. music, sculpture, painting, dance, street art, athletic performance, environmentally conscious and sustainable engineering and architecture - all of these art forms completely bypass the mental realm, and establish a direct, intuitive connection between the artist's true feelings and her audience.

All of those pursuits so "valued" by patriarchy? None of these are art. They all originate in the realm of mentality and have no real meaningfulness. No matter how good a job one does at financial accounting, it will never touch anyone at the level of true feeling, because it originates in mentality. The most precise actuarial calculations aren't art, either. The most efficiently written computer program? The best run office meeting? The most intricately designed military campaign? No, no, and no. The same goes for even the most devious banking plan, the most cost effective nuclear plant, the most productive fracking wells, the shrewdest office politicking, the most insidious bullying ... none of these things could ever be art. They are all about mentality, and false yang and false yin at that. All of these

---

§   This is the challenge and paradox of writing this book: everything here is intended to connect with you on the level of your true visceral feelings via your intuition, yet no matter how impassioned a passage I write, the initial connection with the reader is *de facto* a mental one. I would love for this to be a "Book without Words," but I don't know how to write such a book. Even Felix Mendelssohn's superb *Songs without Words* for solo piano were saddled with annoying names by editors thinking they needed verbal descriptions in order to sell.

pseudo-earth pursuits are about power and control. Feeling, Goddess, and Feminine Love are all about letting go. Try to truly describe falling in love in a written essay. Even the very best authors must resort to analogy to come close to describing what for you is crystal clear. When you have amazing sex, isn't it extraordinarily difficult to describe it in words at all? And if you call it "mind blowing" that is not just a cliché, but is as accurate a verbal description as you could come up with. Try describing in words exactly why you love your family, human or non-human. Do words fail you? You may be able to describe your reactions to love, but verbally describing love itself is impossible. What makes communication that relies exclusively on language so different from the non-verbal transmission of Feeling? It seems the clearer your Feelings are, the harder they are to describe in words. If you are a painter or photographer, how much easier it is to describe an ocean sunset or the aurora than it is to write a description of it. Try to convey to someone why a concert you attended had such incredible "energy" and why the memory still means so very much to you. Like all visceral experiences of true feeling, we may try to describe them with the spoken or written word, but we eventually shrug our shoulders and say "you just had to be there."

The Three Realms of Consciousness: Physicality, Mentality, Feelingality

There are three domains, or what I will call *realms*, of consciousness: the *physical realm* (Physicality), the *mental realm* (Mentality), and the *feeling realm*[¶] (Feelingality). (The english language really needs the word "Feelingality" so I am introducing it here. It is telling that this word has not existed). These three realms of consciousness have corresponding ranges of dimensions:

- Physicality is 1D – 4D (the familiar dimensions of space and time),
- Mentality is 5D – 7D (just like a box), and
- Feelingality is 8D and "higher" (8D+) (how much higher? infinitely higher!)

where "D" is an abbreviation for "dimension". (Whether you consider these to be physical or metaphysical dimensions is immaterial; it is merely a matter of looking at the same reality from slightly different perspectives.) Terms like "higher" or

---

¶If you want to call the feeling realm "spirituality" that's fine, as long as you understand this as atheistic, not theistic, spirituality – closer to what Taoism and Shintoism mean by spirituality. I avoid using the term spirituality in this book because of all of its religious connotations (to the point where atheists who call themselves spiritual are erroneously told by religious people, and even some other atheists, that they are not really atheists, when they are).

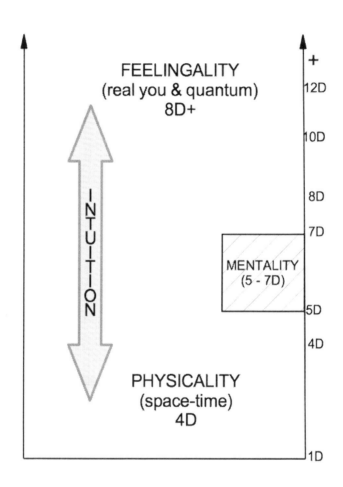

Figure 3.1 - The Three Realms of Consciousness

"above" are misleading. Physicality is qualitatively much "higher" than Mentality, and it is strongly intertwined with Feelingality. I'd prefer to avoid this kind of terminology, but given our language and culture it is hard to describe these things without using "higher/lower" semantics. Figure 3.1 shows the interrelationships of these three realms when they are in their proper perspective, i.e. as they should be. What these realms of consciousness mean to us, how they interact with one another and with us, how we use them, how their disharmony and imbalance affects us, and how we restore them to their proper balance and harmony, is what this book is about.

Physicality is a *realm of action*, but it is a *dependent realm*. The dimensionality of Physicality does not just include the three dimensions of length, width and height, but the time dimension, too (hence it is "4D", not "3D"). The time dimension of physicality is the "clock time" familiar to us in our ordinary waking experience. Physicality is a realm of action because change clearly happens in the physical realm. It is a dependent realm because the change that happens in Physicality depends on the realms of Feeling and Mentality. Physicality will be discussed throughout the chapters of this book.

Mentality, occupying the 5th through 7th dimensions, should be neither more nor less than a toolbox, at our disposal when we need it to create appropriate mental constructs for diverse tasks such as language, computation, and engineering.

Mentality is a realm of the duality of yin and yang, but unlike Physicality, where yin and yang automatically strive toward balance and are always true yin and true yang, there is also false yin and false yang in the mental realm. The consequences of false yin and false yang are profoundly bad, and allow Mentality to run roughshod over Physicality. We've already seen some of the disastrous effects of Mentality under the control of patriarchy in Chapter 1. We will explore Mentality in depth in Chapter 4.

Feelingality is the *realm of Goddess*, the *realm of Love* (the Love we described in Chapter 2), and it is the *realm of Truth*. There is no duality in Feelingality, there is no yin or yang, there is only the fundamental, inseparable unity of Love and Truth. Feelingality spans from the 8th dimension infinitely "upward". Feelingality, the realm of true feeling, is *our* home. Feelingality is the source of our massive creative powers, too. The connection between Physicality and Feelingality is our intuition, and this connection is vital to us. The importance of Feelingality to us, to all of Gaia, and to the universe, cannot be understated. Chapter 5 explores Feelingality in detail, but Feelingality is discussed throughout this book. None of the realms of consciousness can really be considered independently.

Gaia, the living system and consciousness that is the earth Herself and all of Her creatures, is so vitally important to our very existence, and under such terrible threat from patriarchy, that She gets Her own Chapter 6.

Our universe is a quantum universe. The quantum universe is not an exotic realm primarily of interest to physicists, but something we interact with constantly, indeed it has the leading role in what reality we live in. In Chapter 7, we will investigate how we interact with quantum reality, and how we create our reality with the invaluable quantum tools the universe provides us.

In Chapter 8 we'll put everything together, learn what it means to "Just Say Fuck It!", and see why we must say and *do* exactly that to rid ourselves of patriarchy and restore our reality to one of Love, Truth, and Goddess!

Goddess Liberated

Chapter 4

Mentality: Life in a Box

The only way you'll find happiness
is to accept
that the way things are is the way things are.

- The Cow, from *Babe (film)*

If you believe the above quote, you're doomed. Doomed to a miserable life ceded to someone else, someone who has none of your interests at heart, for they are themselves heartless, no matter what they tell you. Our free will is absolute and inviolable, yet like the cow, so many of us give it away, subjugating ourselves to patriarchy and its sham reality. Why do we pretend we need someone else's set of contrived rules and rituals to tell us what is right for us, when each of us *know,* with our in-built intuition, exactly what *is* right for us? Why do we denigrate ourselves, giving away our freedom in exchange for greed masquerading as security, falsehood pretending to be reality, fear disguised as love? Why do so many of us make the cow our totem? We are not sociopaths, we are not the myrmidons and minions orchestrating the patriarchal machine, yet so very many of us march to patriarchy's drumbeat, we get in synch with the sham reality that is handed to us, and stay ... in ... line. So many of us *are* loving and giving by nature, and we *do* want to create a better reality for ourselves and future generations. As children, Truth, Love, connection to our real selves - these were our very nature. What happened to us as adults? As children we naturally and unquestioningly walk the Path.[§] As adults so very many of us tread patriarchy's miry cowpath, entrained in an endless loop of milking after milking after violating milking. We so often choose to follow patriarchy's cow-path because it seems logical. We are surrounded by the life of Gaia, but ensnared by patriarchy's pseudo-reality, and their barren façade seems quite real to us. Patriarchy presents us with a simple syllogism: We live in "the world" (by this, they mean the "world" they've designed for us, of course). Their "world" is a completely mental one. Therefore, to live in their world we must "behave rationally" and "do what is logical" (meaning that we must follow *their* and only their system of "logic" and "rationality"). Above all, they require us to annihilate feeling from our lives, and throw in a good measure of hopelessness to ensure we stay that way. "The only way to find happiness is to accept that the way things are is the way things are." How very much indeed we behave like cows. And we do all of this in exchange for just what, exactly?

[§] "The Tao" = "The Path" or "The Way"; in Taoist philosophy the path of Truth can be (and should be) known but it cannot be described in words

Patriarchal Constructs:
capitalism, religions, and the new age

The most potent weapon of the oppressor
is the mind of the oppressed.
— *Steven Biko*

Obedience, fear, control, hatred, greed, dominance, exploitation; these are patriarchy's hallmarks, and not at all coincidentally these are the core characteristics of capitalist economics, the world's religions, and the "new age movement", too. Take *fear,* for example. Fear means fear of your boss or guru as much as fear of god(s). Despite their ambiguity about almost everything, religions and bosses and gurus make it abundantly clear that you must fear them. You *obey* the god(s) created by religion because you fear what might befall you if you don't. You obey your boss because you fear what will befall you if you don't. You obey the guru because you fear you cannot reach enlightenment without doing it his way. You obey the strictures of the capitalist economic system and religious cults (they are all cults) because of your fear of being cast out by them into the cold unknown if you dare remove yourself from their game. All patriarchal structures are pyramidal - a tiny power elite *controlling* you from the top, controlling everything and everyone, dispensing morsels here and there to keep your *greed* alive but never giving you any real hope of extricating yourself from their total *dominance*. Like the cow, we allow ourselves to be *exploited* "24 X 7", yet not even the cow wears their exploitation like a badge of honor as we do. Once we've been thoroughly wrung out by their feudal system, once nothing remains to eke out of us, patriarchy discards us with nary a thought, happily enjoying each luxury villa and luxury yacht and luxury chalet built from our sweat and blood.

Likewise, religion of any ilk, whether traditional or "new age", regardless of whether it calls itself religion or not, is a mere rusted hulk, just as capitalism is a derelict remnant of any kind of fair economic system. There is no god, there are no gods, and there are no gurus. The only guru is your own inner one, which is your own real-self. Goddess is no god, and there is nothing about Her that even resembles any kind of theism. It may at first seem like a paradox, but Goddess is an utterly atheistic concept. The god guy of religion purports to acknowledge your free will, but then he threatens you with destruction if you actually *follow* your free will. Religions have failed utterly at coercing people to behave morally, themselves behaving immorally at every turn. There are no benevolent dictators, no benevolent religious leaders, no benevolent "spiritual" gurus, either, and assuredly there is no benevolent god-guy. When you exercise your true free will, you beseech no one. You put your "faith" in your own real-self and the quantum universe that supports you. You are kind and caring and nurturing because it *feels* right, and you *know* it is right. You develop the most intimate connections with others who share your embrace of true free will, your love of Truth, indeed your love of Love itself.

It is a little tricky for patriarchy, though. They must keep us sufficiently in fear so we remain enthralled, but not so fearful that we say "enough is enough! Things must change!" At all costs they never want us to get to the point where we seriously consider overthrowing them. This is why they find scapegoats for us to victimize, moreover ensuring that we victimize and oppress one another. "It's us or them!", "you're either with us or against us!", "it's all or nothing!", or "oh, so you're one of *them* [for "*them*" insert *LGBTQ person, Arab, Jew, socialist, anarchist, feminist, atheist, Kurd, tree hugger, Roma, ethnic minority of any kind, intellectual, artist, socialist, ... anyone who might be considered an outsider, anyone exercising their free will, will fit the bill*]." Do you follow your intuition and your true feelings, do you do what you know is right in the face of patriarchy? As any number of indigenous peoples or different-thinking societal groups could attest (though most have not survived to talk about it), following Truth is absolutely anathema to patriarchy and makes you a prime candidate for bullying, torment, torture, and genocide.

I have a term for patriarchy's balancing act of keeping people fearful and naggingly uncomfortable, but not so much so that they'll rise up in revolution. I call it "The Larry Principle". Larry was a former boss of mine some years ago, the owner of a medium-sized business, an entrepreneur who could not have achieved what he did without inheriting his father's business.

Larry seemed perpetually torn between capitalist greed and fits of Feminine compassion. Larry was quite proud of his Principle, which he explained quite succinctly to me: keep the workers focussed on irritations that really don't matter (e.g. a workplace that is too hot or too cold, has glaring fluorescent lighting, is a bit too loud, put people in cubicle land, hold endless nonsensical meetings), so they don't pay any attention to the big things that really do matter (e.g. low wages, promised profit sharing that never happens because those profits are secreted away in offshore tax havens). I respect Larry for his honesty about capitalism, and I pity him that he could never be honest with himself. His wealth kept him addicted to capitalism, his real-self and true feelings emerging, but always just out of his grasp. Was Larry really so very different from most of us? Larry was a compassionate, sensitive, truly Feminine person – he even confided to me once that he was jealous of women because they could experience childbirth but as a man he could not – and yet he was, like all capitalists, enslaved by the very system he served. No, Larry didn't differ from the rest of us very much, except he was able to live his capitalist dream – that is, his capitalist nightmare – more than most of us ever could.

I'm not going to belabor capitalism or religion much longer: read Chapter 1 for a thorough indictment of patriarchy and for a mere sampling of the evils they've wrought. I would be remiss though if I didn't address the "new age" specifically, loosely definable as that term is. The religious overtones of the "new age" are disturbing, misguided, and unsurprising. Despite beginnings that were largely nonconformist and heading down the right path, most of the "new age" milieu now features entrenched greed and capitalism, and thinly veiled, if not outright, religiosity. At their worst the preachers of the "new age" strongly incorporate Christian concepts of god syncretized with Buddhism, remaining comfortably patriarchal (which both of these religions certainly are), their tone dreadfully evocative of American evangelists, no matter how dreamy and reassuring they may sound. These overwhelmingly white, overwhelmingly upper middle class, overwhelmingly male, greedy "new age" preachers have "made it" in every worst capitalistic sense of the word (a capitalism they openly embrace). Their method of "generating abundance" is the tried-and-true method of religious proselytizers through the ages, filling both their egos and their coffers. The "new age" preachers mainly victimize needy, upper middle class white women, promising to fill the void that these women sincerely want to fill, yet these preachers are careful to never offend the status quo, never to challenge anyone very much, and never to really criticize patriarchy ... they are not about to risk losing their income stream. The "new age" often speaks of things like your "higher self" – but doesn't this imply there is something even higher (your "highest self"?), so at best you're still in 2nd position. They speak of "a veil" separating you from your "higher self". If there is a "veil" it is a veil of our own making, and we, and we alone, can lift it. We do not need the help of "new age" gurus or anyone else to "lift the veil" no matter how much their twisted wisdom will cost us. There is no veil!

Preachers of the "new age" hold themselves to be "channels" doing "channeling": distant, superior ("I'm the channel, you're not"), dispensing putative wisdom from on high, these "channels" on the stage run the same swindle as the men sitting in ashrams and monasteries and caves. Most of these "new age" gurus have, of course, become monetarily wealthy, which they openly equate with "abundance". Real abundance has nothing to do with money or things! The "new age" movement is neither revolutionary nor sincere. It doesn't matter that decades ago they may have started out with honest intentions and revolutionary messages, those messages have been diluted and are gone. The "new age" movement has become poisoned and irrelevant. If a "movement" is not revolutionary, does not challenge patriarchy, and is blatantly greedy and capitalist, it is part of the problem, and it is pointless.

Adopting any kind of doctrine means ceding your free will and accepting someone else's control, even if the doctrine you adopt is purportedly atheistic. I've observed atheists behaving as if there is an "atheist orthodoxy", and they even speak about such a notion, but this is a blatant oxymoron in which an atheistic religion is substituted for some other one. You might think "atheistic religion" is itself an oxymoron, but since religion is a completely mental construct, an "atheistic religion" is no more an oxymoron than "capitalist system". Believing in Love, or Truth, or true feeling, is not contradictory to atheism. Atheists who insist there is only a physical 4D world are the same kind of people who would have denied the reality of quantum physics on the same grounds a hundred years ago, and who would have denied evolution a hundred years before that. Denying the existence of anything but what can be observed in 4D space-time is absurd in a world where every year we don't just stretch the boundary of what "physically observed" means, but where it has been unequivocally demonstrated that the very act of observation *determines* the result of what we observe (this is the quantum phenomenon known as the observer effect). We must not just reject religion, but everything that reeks of religion and masquerades as something else, whether that "something else" is "new age" mumbo-jumbo or a purportedly atheistic orthodoxy. We need to be uncompromising in our rejection of any pseudo-reality pretending to be fundamental Truth, no matter the source. And like any bad habit, today is a good day to quit.

Goddess is a fundamentally atheistic concept.

It is ironic that one of the principle arguments for religious- or authority-based morality, is that people will otherwise not behave ethically, when in fact nothing could be further from the truth. Throughout history the least ethical, most untrue, unfeeling, unloving, downright horrid people have found their home in religion and politics. An atheistic morality is a morality based purely on Truth; there is no mental construct intervening between you and your real-self. An anarchic reality is one devoid of patriarchal artifice, there are no structures of pseudo-reality to hide behind. It is unsurprising that some of the *most* moral people in history have been atheists or anarchists, or both. If you find yourself drawn to substitute Goddess worship for god-guy worship, even a little tiny bit, you're missing the point completely. Goddess is physics, not religion, and not some kind of conscious spirit in any patriarchal god-guy sense. If you are already a compassionate atheist, or a secular humanist, and you already say "fuck it!" to patriarchy and mean it, you understand Goddess. I just ask you to keep an open mind as to what constitutes physics, free will, and consciousness. The atheism of Goddess is not compassionless amoral atheism - quite the contrary. Goddess atheism is one of complete individual responsibility. Indeed there are consequences to our choices, and the consequences of some of our bad choices can be severely bad. If you make a bad choice for yourself and only yourself, 100% of your own free will, that is bad for you personally, but you will not be punished, or smitten, or any such thing. Such choices that affect no one and nothing beyond you yourself are, however, quite rare and becoming ever more so. Our interconnectedness is very real and consequential. If you make a bad choice of your own free will that affects other humans, that is bad, and if it hurts the planet, that is even worse. You still will not be punished, or smitten, or anything like that (if the universe worked that way, our planet would be pristine and peaceful by now). Think of having a true friend: do they sit in retrospective judgment over your bad decisions? Do they tell you what you *should* do? Or do they listen with patient understanding and support, regardless of the choices you have made or will make, even if it is perfectly clear to them your choices are or were not so great. Your true friend listens to you with compassion, advises you with her own wisdom, even strongly so, but unwaveringly respects your free will. This is the way it is with Goddess. The decision to do what feels right to you, to follow what your intuition is saying, or instead to ignore your intuition and choose to do what you mentally calculate is somehow the better choice, is yours and only yours. Your true friend does not sit in judgment and smite you, no matter how much your choice or non-choice may pain her. No matter how much it pains Goddess, or Gaia, these concepts are not some kind of personal god-guy armed with lightning bolts and other smiting tools.

Goddess Love is Feminine Love.

Goddess walks you over to the tree and says "eat the apples! Not only are they delicious, they are empowering!" Feminine Love is love that completely embraces and is embraced by true Feeling and true Truth. There may be other things in the Mental realm of pseudo-earth humans call love, but those are not love. If you choose to try and control or limit someone else's free will, you are not in alignment with Goddess. If you go along with controlling and limiting someone's free will, whether you do it actively or tacitly, you are not in alignment with Goddess. If you allow and facilitate someone's free will, advising and helping but not sitting in judgment, then you are in alignment with Goddess. Simple. The opposite of patriarchy and patriarchal hegemony is not matriarchy and matriarchal domination, and matriarchal worship is neither substitute nor solution to patriarchal worship. I must admit it is more than tempting, after thousands of years of patriarchal oppression, to let patriarchy have it and inflict the full fury of the Feminine on the bastards. Well ok it is *really* tempting. But that is not Goddess, and we know that. The antidote to patriarchy is *free will* - and that's it. Notice I didn't say "free will and love and compassion and truth" or anything like that. Why? Because all of these attributes, no matter how much we are intuitively certain of what is right, must originate in a free will decision to do the right thing, a free will decision made by each one of us, alone. Isn't that empowering? Creating for good because you and you alone decide by your own free will that this is the right thing to do: now that *is* empowerment!

Mentality, thought-forms, and pseudo-realities

The "world" in which we perceive we live - what metaphysicians sometimes call the "earth-plane" - is a *pseudo-reality* ruled by and subject to Mentality and the rules of mental "logic". There is nothing inherently "good" or "bad" about a pseudo-reality, no more than there is anything inherently "good" or "bad" about Mentality. A pseudo-reality is a blank canvas upon which we paint a "world" in which we spend almost all of our waking life, just as Mentality, when in its proper position and used in its intended role, is at our service.

Before we continue discussing the implications of Mentality and pseudo-realities on our perceived world, here are some key definitions:

- A *thought* is a thought. We'll make this axiomatic and our starting point. A thought is individual, and it is transient.

- A *thought-form,* unlike a thought, has persistence. Like a thought, a thought-form is also individual.

- A *mental-construct* is a group of thought-forms that is logically consistent from a mental point-of-view (and only from a mental point-of-view).[§] A mental-construct is also individual.

- A *pseudo-reality* is a collection of mental-constructs that are

  - purely mental - there is nothing *intrinsically real* about them, they are neither Physically real, nor are they real in the realm of Feeling,

  - logically consistent from a purely mental perspective,

[§] at this point you might be wondering what kind of logic is *not* mental, and the answer is profound: the logic of the universe itself is decidedly quantum, not mental. We explore this reality throughout this book.

- ○ adhered to by more than one person (and usually many people), and

- ○ held to be "true" by its adherents (a pseudo-reality maintained by only one person is psychosis, unless that person is very wealthy and powerful, in which case it is called "brilliance").

- *Materialism* is an expression of pseudo-reality, *not* physical reality

How many people do you need to create a mental construct? Not very many at all. In my family, my spouse once accidentally called a sea gull a penguin. This was an expressed thought form. It was really funny, and my entire family began jokingly calling sea gulls, penguins, and penguins, sea gulls. Ten years later, if anyone in our family calls a sea gull a sea gull, we think they are referring to a penguin! Within our family, this has become a full-fledged mental-construct. Of course outside of our family, there is no collective agreement on this mental-construct, so if we call a sea gull a sea gull, people really will think we are talking about sea gulls, demonstrating the ephemeral nature of mental constructs. The word is not the thing it represents;[§] word meanings are very fluid: not only do they change over time, but they differ significantly from person to person, and for a given

---

[§] For a thorough treatment on the subject of language as mental construct I recommend the excellent book *Language in Thought and Action* by S. I. Hayakawa (note he does not call it "mental-construct" but he describes the workings of what I mean by mental-construct very well). This textbook has been in print for more than 70 years.

person they change with time (a dictionary is merely an historical snapshot of word meanings agreed upon by a few experts). Imagine you are a biologist, and you hear the word "cell". Most likely the first thing that comes to mind is the building block of organic life. Now imagine you are a biologist sent to a government gulag and someone says the word "cell". Will your emotional reaction to the word have changed?

My linguistic example of penguins and sea gulls is innocuous and fun, but mental-constructs can be much, much bigger. Like words, languages themselves are mental-constructs. Humans are expert at creating mental-constructs, but we don't stop there. We erect entire societal structures around pseudo-realities. Pseudo-realities can and should serve us well, providing a framework for our waking life, but they just as easily are co-opted for nefarious purposes. That is what has happened here on a grand, grand scale. The massive pseudo-realities of religion and capitalism, including the hatred, greed and materialism that are their part-and-parcel, have been and are devastating the planet. These pseudo-realities, imposed by the very few on the very many, are guaranteed to be corrupt, debilitating, harmful, and far worse.[¶] Capitalism itself is a kind of grand fusion of feudalism and religion. It requires you to believe in it, to live in fear if you don't believe in it, and to pledge yourself in indentured servitude to not just the system, but to the ridiculously small group of

---

[¶] Authoritarian centrally-planned economies arose, briefly flourished, and became virtually extinct during the course of the 20th century. They are no longer relevant, other than as a tool capitalists and religionists use to make you fear overturning their systems.

patriarchs who are at the very top of its pyramid of mass oppression. Of course the capitalist pseudo-realities, like religious and totalitarian pseudo-realities, want us to lose hope and believe that they are so almighty we cannot change them or stop them, but that is absurd. When we fall into this trap we are forgetting the fundamentally simple underpinning of these massive pseudo-realities: religion and capitalism and their ilk are all built on a house of cards of mental constructs which have no intrinsic reality or value whatsoever! The word or thought-form or mental-construct or pseudo-reality is not the thing. You can point to a carrot and prove it is intrinsically real. Regardless of what you call it, a carrot is physically real in 4D space-time. A carrot *is* the thing. You *feel* Love, and just as certainly as the carrot, you *know* Love is intrinsically real. Love is intrinsically real because it originates in, indeed it "lives in" Feelingality, the realm of true feeling. Now consider money. Is it intrinsically real? Of course not. Try feeding your pet rabbit a few dollars or Euros instead of carrots. Can money create Love? Can you exchange money for Love? You can exchange it for a lot of empty things pretending to substitute for Love, but none of these are real. Money, indeed the entire banking and monetary system, is nothing more than a massive, deliberately constructed pseudo-reality. Stage magicians understand perfectly how to create a pseudo-reality. Bankers and stock brokers and swindlers understand how to create pseudo-reality in precisely the same way stage magicians do. Is the recipe for your favorite dish the dish itself? If you believe that, you will starve, just as you are starved by capitalism and religion. The god-guy in all of his incarnations (including polytheistic ones), the archons, religious strictures, capitalist economies - these are *all* mere pseudo-realities based on mental constructs, and nothing more.

The Mentality Box and Pseudo-Earth

Mentality is a box. Metaphysically speaking, it occupies the 5th through 7th dimensions. It should be a toolbox, at our disposal when we need it, and neither more nor less than that. As a metaphysical interface between the realm of Physicality (occupying the 1st through 4th dimensions, i.e. space-time) and the 8th and higher dimensions of Feelingality, the Mentality toolbox is available for our use: to measure, to calculate, to build things for the mutual benefit of us and all of Gaia, to construct *appropriate* mental-constructs (e.g. languages, mathematics), and to create pseudo-realities that harmonize with the intrinsic realities of Feelingality and Physicality (e.g. truly moral and fair economic and social systems). The mental realm, however, is particularly vulnerable to attack and misuse. Like the physical realm, Mentality is also a realm of duality, but unlike Physicality, where there is a natural, self-correcting balance of true yin and true yang (e.g. Gaia), Mentality is the only one of the three realms of consciousness where false yang and false yin can intrude and take hold. Mentality must be kept in check, always under the guidance and oversight of our true feeling-self of

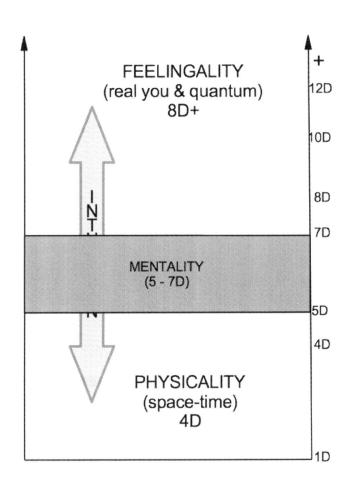

Figure 4.1 - Distorted Mentality Box cuts off our intuition

Feelingality, or it can easily be co-opted for ill purpose, becoming bloated out of all proper proportion, taking on inappropriate roles for which it was never intended. When Mentality is in its proper place and perspective, it is the "toolbox" of Figure 3.1.

When Mentality is completely out-of-whack, however, it is the Pandora's box of Figure 4.1, and this is where we find ourselves today. We are enmeshed in a distorted pseudo-reality, engineered by patriarchal sociopaths, a pseudo-reality so massive it has become *pseudo-earth*. In pseudo-earth, Mentality has become so enormous that it is a barrier between the intrinsic realities of Physicality and Feelingality, cutting us off from our true feelings, and thus cutting us off from our real selves. In pseudo-earth the physical realm is mercilessly dominated by patriarchy. Mentality is a barrier between our 4D-selves of Physicality and our real-selves of Feelingality.

Let's look inside the Mentality Box (Figure 4.2). We see that there is a chasm - an unbreachable chasm - splitting Mentality. One easy way to understand this is using the Taoist concept of duality, **yin** and **yang**. Some readers may already be familiar with the concept of yin and yang, but there are widely held misconceptions about yin and yang that must be cleared up. Yin and yang are not "opposites" in the Western sense, nor do they mean "male" or "female" in any Western sense, either. Most translations of the *Tao Te Ching* or *I Ching* are written from a patriarchal viewpoint, leading the reader to conclude syllogisms along the lines of "yin is bad, yin is female, therefore female is bad", or "yang is good, yang is male, therefore male is good".

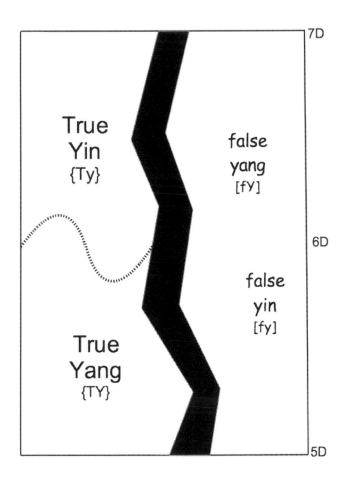

Figure 4.2 - Inside the Mentality Box

This misinformation, or disinformation, is unsurprising but horribly wrong, not just because it perpetuates a gender binary which does not exist, but it is not what Taoists intended by these concepts. Most interpretations of yin and yang are also completely missing a crucial concept: that of *true yin* and *true yang* vs. *false yin* and *false yang*. True yin and true yang, which I will symbolically refer to as {Ty/TY}, form harmonized, complementary pairs. It is easier to define {Ty/TY} by giving some examples rather than trying to define them explicitly. Strength (e.g. protecting your family, protecting the earth, standing up for humans' and Gaia's rights) is an attribute of true yang. Flexibility and receptivity (e.g. being compassionate, nurturing, and understanding) is the true yin complement to true yang. Thus strength and flexibility form a complementary {Ty/TY} pair. When the Tao speaks of "firmness in flexibility, flexibility in firmness", this is what is meant. Wisdom and enlightenment can be true yin or true yang attributes depending on how they are used. True yin and true yang form countless beautiful complementary pairs, and instruct us in living a fulfilled, abundant life. Being complementary pairs, it is not possible to have one without the other and to still have *true* yin and *true* yang.

The fundamental, complementary relationship of {Ty/TY} is often depicted symbolically in the "yin/yang diagram" at the center of the bagua, where we see true yin and true yang as not just separate and distinct attributes, but fully *embodying each other* in the "dots" as shown in the diagram of Figure 4.3, in which flexibility is embodied in firmness, and firmness is embodied in flexibility:

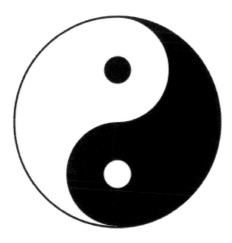

Figure 4.3 - Yin/Yang Diagram at the center of the Bagua

False yin and false yang, which I symbolize [fy] and [fY] respectively, do *not* form complementary pairs, nor do they in any way "balance" each other. There are no pairings that are [fy]/[fY]. Take, for example, dominance and aggression, which are false yang attributes. Submission, subservience and co-dependency are false yin. There are *not*, however, false yin, false yang pairings like aggression/subservience, or dominance/submission. False yin and false yang characteristics just constitute a chaotic list of false attributes anathema to living a fulfilled, meaningful, *real* life. When we exhibit, or worse, embrace [fy] and [fY] attributes such as materialism, we endure an unfulfilled, meaningless existence, and our "life", such as it is, is not true to our real selves; we are divorced from the beautiful, feeling, compassionate creators who we truly are. There is no getting around it: living a life in false yin and false yang is living a life of falsehood, and living a life of falsehood is a life wasted and un-lived. Nor are there ever pairings *between* true and false attributes, either: there are no pairs like {Ty}/[fY], or [fy]/{TY}. For example, true strength, a true yang attribute, does not and cannot form a pair with weakness, which is false yin. The real duality, the only real duality, is between true yin and true yang, {Ty/TY}.

There is an unbreachable chasm in the Mental realm between {true yin/true yang} and [false yin], [false yang].

True yin and true yang are *inherent* to Physicality. In the 4D physical realm of space-time, (1) true yin and true yang are in natural balance, and (2) if out of balance, they *automatically* strive to balance each other (e.g. Gaia's immune system). When Physicality is connected to Feelingality via our intuition (see Figure 3.1), this balance remains undisturbed, with any small perturbation in the {Ty/TY} balance easily correcting itself.

Indeed, Feelingality is the source of balance for Physicality. As we will explore in Chapter 5, this is because the realm of feeling is the unity of Truth and Love (there are no {Ty/TY} pairs in Feelingality as {Ty/TY} is meaningless in this realm). A major problem arises in Physicality, however, when it becomes subjected to the false yin and false yang side of the Mentality box, a Mentality so completely corrupted and devastated as the one patriarchy has engineered and in which the planet finds herself hostage.

In patriarchy's pseudo-earth, Mentality has been deliberately and mercilessly employed to keep the {Ty/TY} of Physicality imbalanced, but remember, true yin and true yang in Physicality *must* strive to return to balance. The results are the increasingly violent self-corrections we are experiencing on the planet, whether they are upheavals in the natural world or in human societies. This is simply how Gaia's "immune system" must function, and how it does function. Things would be bad enough if patriarchy and their minions went along in their own pseudo-reality apart from the rest of us, but our situation here is dire. Patriarchy has managed to impose an entire pseudo-earth on the planet, effectively cutting off almost the entire physical realm from Feelingality, thus forcing the planet's immune system to kick into higher and higher gear. This means patriarchy is indeed the source of its own demise. Unfortunately, this also means patriarchy is very close on being the source of our demise, too.

Eras of Pseudo-Earth, and Reclaiming our Reality

The pseudo-earth under which we exist is no place for the Feminine, where it should be the *portal* to the Feminine. Consider this statement from the *Tao Te Ching:*[§]

> When the Tao itself was lost, its qualities remained;
>
> When its qualities were lost, compassion remained;
>
> When compassion was lost, customs remained;
>
> When customs were lost, disorder remained. The beginning of stupidity.

Pseudo-earth should be the infrastructure of our 4D reality. Instead, as it has been engineered and run by patriarchy, pseudo-earth is our infra-*destructure*. It was not always this way,

---

[§]   Adapted from Lao Tzu, *Tao Te Ching*, J. Legge (translator), Sacred Books of the East (1891), Vol. 39, Ch. 38
Original text as translated by Legge:
"When the Tao was lost, its attributes appeared;
when its attributes were lost, benevolence appeared;
when benevolence was lost, righteousness appeared;
and when righteousness was lost, the proprieties appeared. Propriety is the attenuated form of leal-heartedness and good faith, and is also the commencement of disorder; swift apprehension is (only) a flower of the Tao, and is the beginning of stupidity."

it does not have to be this way, it should not be this way, and we must do all we can to return it to what it should be.

In the oldest of days, our pseudo-earth was in complete harmony with the 8D+ realm of Feelingality, and with Gaia. Pseudo-earth was Feminine and Goddess-centric. This was the **Goddess Era** where there was not even a division into true yin/true yang. This was the era of the Tao, a time when true feeling, the unity of Truth and Love in the Tao, was seamlessly integrated with pseudo-earth. We can figuratively represent this era with an azure blue sky. This was a very, very long time ago. Memory of its peoples are lost, and their cultural artifacts have vanished, too.

The **Era of Duality** ensued. This was not so very different from the "Goddess Era" but pseudo-earth moved from unity to duality. This was still an era where the Feminine prevailed in all of our interactions with one another as well as with Gaia. In this era the "Tao itself was lost" and its attributes appeared, i.e. the duality of true yin and true yang. The Era of Duality was still a time where pseudo-earth consisted purely of true yin and true yang; no false attributes had entered yet. Figuratively, the sky was a crystal clear blue by daylight, and an inky blackness by night.

There was no moment in time when things suddenly switched to the hyper-masculine, patriarchal pseudo-reality of today. There was considerable geographical variation, but evidence from antiquity in regions such as Asia Minor show a Goddess-centric worldview was still firmly in place as recently as 3500 to 8000 years ago.[¶] This means that for virtually all of the nearly 6 million years of human history, the prevailing pseudo-reality was nurturing, comforting, and Love-based, in harmony with Goddess and Gaia. If human history is likened to a 24 hour day, the eras where Goddess and the Feminine prevailed lasted for the first 23 hours and 53 minutes of that day. There wasn't a hint then of any "veil" separating us from our real selves, nor of servitude to anyone, nor worship of anything. Mentality was kept in its proper perspective. We felt and intuited Goddess, we "knew" Her intimately, and just as intimately, we knew our own real, true selves. While our ancient sisters and brothers did not necessarily comprehend quantum reality intellectually, that was immaterial: they *felt* quantum and higher dimensions, and in a real sense they understood quantum viscerally and in far greater depth than we do today.

It was during the ***Era of Differentiation*** that things began to head downhill. Even in the older days, from about 4500 to 3500 years ago, most people were still Goddess-centric, and everyone would have not only known of Goddess and the Feminine, they would have taken these truths for granted. Figuratively during this era, there were thick clouds amassing on the horizon of a sky still so clear and blue by day, and inky black

---

¶ Helga Kaiser, "Gott Weiblich: Eine verborgene Seite des biblischen Gottes", *welt und umwelt der bibel*, 2/2008

by night, that their presence went largely unnoticed. Pseudo-earth was compassionate, innocent, welcoming, open - and vulnerable. This was the era where "the qualities of the Tao were lost, but compassion remained". While Mentality was still held in check, this was the first era when false yin and false yang appeared. Patriarchy arose, covert and cunning, during the Era of Differentiation. Given the innocent and trusting nature of the Feminine, patriarchy had no trouble marching in. How or why this happened is beyond the scope of the present book, but happen it did.

Things went to shit after that, during the **Era of Deception**. Goddess was rapidly degraded throughout this era, from about 3500 to 2500 years ago, and this is the era when the god-guy began to rear his hideous head. Patriarchy were putting their odious plan into action. What was worse, patriarchy established "Goddess worship", which was deliberately patterned after god-guy worship. The truth of Goddess rapidly was lost to most, including the essential truth that she was not to be worshipped! "Compassion was lost, [only] customs remained." During this Era of Deception, Mentality began to swell out of all proportion to its proper role, and false yin and false yang began to dominate the mental realm. Physicality found itself plunged more and more into enslavement to Mentality. Like so many colonial powers wiping out indigenous peoples, pockets of resistance to patriarchy were sought out and eradicated. Only a very few of us managed to move "underground", often to remote locales such as Scandinavia, Iceland, the Celtic lands of the British Isles and Brittany in northwestern France, the region of modern Bhutan and Tibet, and among a few indigenous tribes of New Zealand, Australia, Oceania, and the Americas (e.g. the Anasazi and Hopi). We preserved some collective memory, however imperfect, of the way things truly are and how they truly should be. In less than a millennium we found our figurative sky plunged into an era of murky patriarchal overcast, and the ruling class replete with sociopaths.

Beginning worldwide about 2500 years ago, we find ourselves in the ***Era of Chaos.*** "Disorder reigns" and we are well past "the beginning of stupidity". This era of a pseudo-earth of fear, greed, repression, and patriarchal obedience, grips us to this day. Patriarchy's dreary overcast has devolved into a full-fledged storm in our figurative sky, actively attacking the Feminine, women, children, LGBTQ people, Gaia, anyone who dares to not succumb to or even question patriarchy's system of bondage and servitude. Mentality became bloated out of all proper proportion, at best forming a thick filter between Physicality and Feelingality, but most often, dominated by irrational false yin and false yang. Mentality has erected a seemingly impenetrable barrier to our real selves. For the past 2500 years, it has been very bleak for the Feminine and Goddess.

But it is impossible, of course, for patriarchy to wipe out Goddess, no more than they can erase the Truth or Love that is the quantum universe itself. Patriarchy's twisted pseudo-reality may still dominate human consciousness, but our free will remains, and our free will, for lack of a better term, is sacred and immutable. We may still find ourselves drowning in the Era of Chaos, but we also find ourselves in the **Era of Hope**. And some of us *do* exercise our free will for Love, and Truth. Some of us *are* standing up to patriarchy, and standing up *for* Gaia and Goddess. Some of us recognize Truth, more of us recognize the true feeling of Love, and a few of us not only recognize Truth and Love but we are *acting* on it. We may still be few, but we are a notable, crucial, essential few and our numbers are geometrically increasing. We have the greatest, most peaceful "weapon" of all, a "weapon" that is completely inaccessible to patriarchy: the quantum universe. We may take what seem like "baby steps" in our lives, but whenever we put Mentality back in its box and use it as the toolbox it should be, whenever we stand up for human rights and human dignity and human equality, whenever we do whatever we can to protect and defend Gaia and Her creatures, when we do any of these things at the smallest or greatest personal sacrifice, it is in all of these times we engage the quantum universe, we blow patriarchy away, and we usher in the Era of Hope. Our importance and impact is immeasurable. Whenever we act from Love and Truth simply *because* it is the right thing to do, when we express Feminine Love because it *feels* right, it is then that we still patriarchy's attacking storms.

It is then that we rend gaps in patriarchy's obscuring cloud cover. We are like a tsunami: barely detectable at first, building tremendous energy, then suddenly manifesting unparalleled power as we slam into the shore of patriarchy. When we and our actions reach a level of criticality, patriarchy will be left dumbfounded, and they will not know what hit them. Unmistakably, unstoppably, and inevitably, azure blue skies are peeking through. We are reclaiming our reality, constructing, bit by bit, the pseudo-earth that *should* be. Goddess *is* returning, for we are *being* Goddess.

Chapter 5

Feelingality

we are beings of feeling

We may spend our conscious lives in the physical realm, we may grossly overuse and misuse our mentality, but truly, we are beings of feeling. In Feelingality we are unabashedly, unequivocally, undeniably, *us*. The realm of feeling is our home.

Love and Her twin sister, Truth, comprise
an inseparable, fundamental unity.

There *is* absolute Truth, and there *is* absolute Love. Love and Truth are not in any way a duality; they constitute an inseparable unity. Indeed, they are *the fundamental unity*: there can neither be Truth without Love, nor Love without Truth.

Feelingality is the realm of Love and Truth.

Our home in the realm of feeling is the home of Love and Truth, too! The consequences of this are profound. Freed from the space-time restrictions of Physicality, stripped of the baggage and burden of Mentality, we are, in Feelingality, *truly us:* we are infinite in dimensions far beyond our rational comprehension, each one of us an extraordinarily powerful creator-goddess in our own right, yet each of us also an integral part of ineffable Goddess. In our home, we are intertwined with the fundamental unity that is Love and Truth, we are entangled with the quantum universe, and we comprise an integral part of Goddess Herself. This means our true, feeling-self is not just indescribably powerful, but she is unwaveringly and uncompromisingly honest. In Feelingality, our free will is our *true* free will, unerringly creating what is best for each of us, for humanity, for Gaia and for the universe. In the realm of feeling we are incapable of being misguided into creating anything that is harmful or injurious. In the realm of true feeling we eat the delicious, succulent fruit of the tree of knowledge, and we thus gain *true* enlightenment, that is, *the enlightenment of feeling*.[§] When patriarchal constructs like religion and capitalism denigrate and demonize true feeling, they attack our real selves and our true enlightenment, for they know that once we get

---

[§]Are you are still guilty or caught up about eating "the fruit of the tree of knowledge" in the first place? I congratulate you on reading this book and urge you to read on! You are liberating yourself.

even a small taste of who we truly are in Feelingality, we are indeed unstoppable.

While our creative power seems to be latent in 4D Physicality, from the perspective of the reality of 8D+ Feelingality, our creations are real and *already* exist. Our true feeling-self comprises *all* realities, and from the perspective of Feelingality, the 8D+ perspective, *none of these realities are potential - they all already exist.*[∞] All realities are real and manifest, we just don't have 4D access to them. There are many realities, which we can equally call "universes", spanning from 4D Physicality through the 8D+ dimensions of Feelingality. There are some realities/universes where we exist in 4D space-time, and many other realities/universes in which we do not exist in Physicality, but our real-self in 8D+ exists across *all* realities/universes. There are those Physical realities in which 4D-us, and our 4D circumstances, are much like our "current" ones, and there are those in which we and our 4D circumstances are quite different from how we consciously perceive ourselves. From the perspective of 8D+ Feelingality, terms like "past life" or "future life" really make no sense. Importantly, this means there *are* realities in which our 4D-selves inhabit 4D space-time that *is* Goddess-centric and rooted in Love and Truth. There are realities in which patriarchy plays no role whatsoever, because

---

∞ In Chapter 7, Quantum, we delve into how the 4D idea of "existence" coupled with our ordinary experience of clock time is inaccurate and unreliable in the quantum universe. For now it is important to note that when we say all realities "already exist" this does not mean they all exist at the same "time" in the ordinary way we mean time, but they do already exist in the sense of higher-dimensional quantum reality.

patriarchy does not exist at all! These realities, whose projections into 4D Physicality are based on Love and Truth, whose 5D~7D Mentality is kept in its proper place and perspective, realities permeated by the Feminine Love of Goddess, are not just some kind of esoteric, theoretical realities. These realities/universes are every bit as real as whichever particular reality we find ourselves immersed in at any given moment. Clearly, these are the realities and universes we, and all of Gaia and our planet, *want* to live in. These are the realities in which we are *meant* to live! But how do we gain access to them in our "ordinary lives" of 4D Physicality? (There are times we *do* encounter these other realities - when we dream, for example, or during peak experiences - but we do not ordinarily have conscious access to them). It is well and good that our real feeling-self has access to these far better realities, but what about 4D-us? How do we change universes/realities so we can flourish in a reality of Truth, Love and Goddess?

Consider what our true feelings really are: a synergy of our true feelings in *all* realities, encompassing all of these realities, yet independent of any associated 4D space-time Physicality we experience.

Our feeling-self is an 8D+ infinity
spanning and encompassing all realities/universes.
Our feeling-self is fully aware of all of these realities/universes.

Our true feeling-self *experiences* all of these realities, no matter how "distant" or different they may be from our present 4D one. You could say our feeling-self is omniscient. This is why our true feeling-self is immutably honest and infallible: our feeling-self "sees" everything! This also means our true feeling-self has limitless creative power, including the power to "relocate" us to a Goddess-centric, Feminine, Love-based, Truth-based universal reality, with a matching physical reality in 4D space-time.

What does it really mean to say "we create our reality"? When we truly create, when we create from our true, Love-based feelings in 8D+ Fcelingality, we are not really creating anything new at all! We are in fact shifting, moving, relocating to another universe/reality. If you really think about it, "creating our own reality" sounds daunting and unattainable, even preposterous. It would be like building a new house in the same place as your present house without even knocking the old house down. When we realize that "creating our reality" really means relocating to a different reality that already exists, it is like leaving where you currently live and moving somewhere better: plausible, feasible, and completely doable! Nevertheless, I will continue using the terms "creating" and "creation" because from the 4D perspective, what we do feels like we are "creating our reality" and not just "relocating to a new reality". It is only from the perspective of an "outside observer" - the perspective our 8D+ feeling-self has, but our 4D physical-self does not - that we clearly see that what we are really doing is moving to another, already-extant reality. (We do not need to worry about moving to a reality/universe that is worse than the one we already have, because our Love- and

Truth-based feeling-self unwaveringly guides us to a better reality/universe). From the perspective of Feelingality-us, moving to a new reality/universe seems easy, as indeed it is. From the point-of-view of Physicality-us, creating our reality/universe seems incredibly daunting, even though Feelingality-us knows better. The key is to get Physicality-us connected to and synchronized with Feelingality-us. And here is the *really* good news: the infrastructure for doing this already exists! It is called our intuition.

Intuition

This book is indeed a "how to" book, where "how to" means how to restore and reinvigorate the vital intuitive link between physical-us and feeling-us. We naturally and unquestioningly operate from intuition when we are children. We intuitively know what is right and what is wrong, we are certain what is fair and what is unfair, all without any intrusion from religion or external moralizing structures. We know what is right because we *feel* what is right, and our intuition translates our true-feeling into action in the physical world. As we age, a mentality-obsessed world chips away at us until our innate intuitive connection to our real-self erodes to nothingness (in Taoist tradition, this is said to begin in earnest when you are about 16 years old). It is little wonder that patriarchy's mental world spends so much effort besmirching the value of intuitive thought, derisively devaluing "feminine intuition" at every opportunity. It is paradoxical that what mentality-driven society labels "childlike innocence" is in fact the highest level of intuition, the true enlightenment and wisdom inherent in each of us. It is tragic that patriarchy pretends to admire this "innocence", but then they beat it out of us.

Consider the "top five regrets of the dying"[§] compiled a few years ago by an Australian palliative care nurse who collected the thoughts of many of her patients who were close to death. They said they wished they'd had the courage to live lives that were true to themselves, rather than what was expected of them. They wished they had not worked so hard. The dying wished they were courageous enough to express their feelings! They wished they had let themselves be happier. None of their top regrets mentioned acquiring more money and things, and of course they called on neither god nor religion. Each of these dying wishes hearken back to the time when we happily let our intuition guide our life. It seems, sadly, that for too many of us, our intuitive connection to our real feeling-self is finally restored on our deathbed, but that is of course far too late. And there is no salvation awaiting us: we obsolesce our intuition at our great peril. If you've chosen to live a cowardly, materialist, untrue, unfulfilled, unfeeling, unhappy life, there really is no getting around the fact that your life has been a tragic waste, and worse still if you inflicted harm on Gaia or other people.

----

§Bronnie Ware quoted by Susie Steiner, "Top 5 regrets of the dying", *The Guardian* (1 February 2012)

But if you are reading this book, chances are very high that the preceding paragraph does *not* apply to you. You *are* someone seeking the path of a meaningful, fulfilled life. Like so many of us, you simply need to revitalize and restore your intuition. At its most fundamental level,

Restoring our intuition means un-growing up!

When we regain our childhood sense of wonder, we prepare ourselves to restore our intuition. When we once again see the world through the crystal clear lens of our so-called "childlike innocence", we begin to restore the supreme wisdom that is our intuition. We know that our intuition is innate within us, but we must re-learn how to listen to, and heed, our intuition when it "speaks" to us. Once we put ourselves back together, using our intuition to reunite 4D Physicality-us with 8D+ Feelingality-us, it is then that we begin to take real, no-turning-back action in our lives. In Taoist terms, we "empty the mind" when we clear out the dross of Mentality which has been acting as a poor and dishonest substitute for our intuition. We "fill the belly" when we restore our intuition. True abundance has nothing to do with accumulating things, exercising control, or any other of patriarchy's falsehoods. Sustenance has nothing to do with ego fulfillment; our true, feeling-self has no ego. True abundance and sustenance is "filling the belly" with our inherent intuition, being truly alive once again, and adhering to the unwaveringly honest wisdom with which our real feeling-self supplies us. It is when we live a life guided by our intuition that we can proudly, happily, joyously know we are living a fulfilled, active, truly abundant life.

Can we bypass our intuition? Or perhaps we can employ an intercessor to do the job for us? After all, the latter is what religions, capitalism, "new age" gurus, and all their ilk promise they can do for us ... so we know we can dismiss that notion out of hand. But sincerely, what about cultivating a direct connection with our feeling-self? Why can't we just bypass our intuition and always be directly "in touch" with our 8D+ feeling-self? Wouldn't that make everything simpler? Unfortunately this is problematic. We do live almost all of our waking lives in the physicality of 4D space-time, so any 8D+ information has to be "stepped down" to be useful to us at the physical level. (Denying our physicality - the wont of so many mystics - is as much denying an essential part of who we are, as is denying our real, feeling-selves.)

Though we may hope otherwise, we might as well assume, and *act,* as if we are supposed to be here, experiencing this particular physical reality. The rare occasions when we bypass our intuition and we *consciously,* directly unite with our real feeling-self, such as during peak experiences or in deep meditation, are indeed energizing, but they are inevitably short-lived. These rare occurrences provide scant long-term relief from the mire of physical and mental existence, let alone provide any real respite from patriarchy's pseudo-earth. We humans are bent on trying to induce more frequent and prolonged peak experiences, e.g. through the adrenalin rush of extreme sports, insincere sex, or drug abuse. We do this not so much to escape

Physicality as to earnestly try and maintain the longest possible connection with our real feeling-selves. Healthy peak experiences should be fun and inspirational, they should give us insight into our real selves, they should recharge our figurative batteries, but they cannot solve the "problem" of Physicality for us. The ecstatic state is not sustainable in our 4D physical lives, at least if we want to remain sane and engaged with humanity and with Gaia. Physicality inevitably intrudes, we "come back to earth", or even crash back into Physicality, and we find ourselves glumly re-planted in 4D Physicality.

So is our best option to just keep escaping Physicality by any means possible? Or perhaps we must simply "grin and bear it" à la Catholic and Jewish custom? Escapism inevitably leads us to our physical demise, with the terrible side effect of losing touch with the very intuition we should be cultivating. Along with ignoring our intuition, the latter course could only make sense if there were an utopian "afterlife". Alas there is no afterlife, utopian or otherwise. Remember, we *are* powerful creator goddesses, and in our Feelingality home we *know* we have limitless creative power! We know in our truest, innermost selves that we are *not* here to give up - quite the contrary. Our intuition is clearly *the* key for accessing our boundless creative power.

How do we know when we *are* using our intuition? Simple:

If it *feels* right, it *is* right.

If it *feels* wrong, it *is* wrong.

If you think it maybe feels right, but you're unsure, this means your Mentality is blocking your communications with your real-self. It could be a slight blockage, or a near total one, but in either case it is easy enough to overcome if you just listen to *you* and feel your feelings. You might be blocking your intuition out of pseudo-earth fear ("This job is killing me, but I can't afford to quit my job"), or you might be considering taking a path you know doesn't feel right out of fear and deliberate blindness ("I've been offered this great-paying job with this sleazy company, but that doesn't matter, I'll put the money to good use"), but in either case you have failed your intuition, it has not failed you. Fear and doubt of your own intuition are part and parcel of patriarchy's version of pseudo-earth; there is no better weapon in their arsenal for derailing you from what your very own self is telling you is the right or ethical choice. There are some tools to help you get in touch with your real-self and make it easier for you to feel your true feelings, such as the *I Ching,* and some forms of meditation. A healthy diet, exercise, music, art, being in direct contact with nature, all of these are helpful for removing some of the circumstances causing your fear, and thus they help you to again feel your true feelings. But there is no magical solution, no one to pray to, no substitute for *you* being completely honest with *you,* allowing *your* intuition to engage and guide *you* because it simply *feels* right.

A simple indicator of when we are "doing it right" is how patriarchy and their minions respond to our actions. When we are derided by patriarchy for taking right action, then we can be certain we are are using our intuition. When we do what is right because it feels right, when we don't allow mental-us to intervene, we are assuredly using our intuition. When we are guided by our *inner* voice to being the creative, moral, wise beings we truly are, no matter the consequences, we know positively that it is our own intuition guiding us. We should bear in mind, however, that those occasions where our intuition guides us to make enormous "quantum leaps" are rare. Almost all of the time, using our intuition means using our intuition in baby steps. The latent "energy" embodied in our physical-selves connecting intuitively with our 8D+ real-selves is so unimaginably powerful, so incomprehensibly pervasive, and it launches such a cascade of enabling quantum processes, that *our baby steps make a huge difference!* Our baby steps *matter*. I cannot overstate how essential and effective taking intuition-based baby steps is on changing our reality, helping all of humanity, and nurturing the restoration of Gaia. Think of the tiny baby steps, baby steps of a single person or a very few people working together, that launched the Algerian revolution, the *Montagsdemonstrationen* in the former East Germany, the protests of Taksim Square, or the Occupy movement. Not all of these movements may appear to have "succeeded" very much, and patriarchy may smugly believe that they roundly defeated us, but nothing could be further from the truth. We have tremendous creative power as individuals - imagine what our power is like when even a few of us work together! When we work together we really do relocate to realities/universes where things are very much better. These realities are not just within our grasp, they already exist! We just have to move there. It really would only take a relatively small "critical mass" of people to eradicate patriarchy and their pseudo-reality. (It is difficult to say how many people would constitute a "critical mass" but it is on the order of tens of millions, no more than that). This "critical mass" of us following our intuition and coordinating our intuitive-based actions would be like releasing a cascade of energy from a nuclear fusion reaction, but far more powerful than that. A reality under the warm caress of Feminine Love is well within our grasp. A universe of Goddess, of Truth and Love, nourished by true Feeling and guided by intuition based on that true Feeling, is not so far away as we think. A reality of Love is really the ultimate simplicity. Think about how Love works - it doesn't "work" at all! *Love does not ask "why?" Love just is.*

Creating

We find such myriad ways to be creative, it is shocking we would even doubt the power of our own creativity. Why? Because it puts *you* in touch with *you*, and thus by creating, you intimately connect with your real-self via your intuition. There is no more powerful way for you to do this than when you create, for when you truly create, your limitless power is coupled with your free will, and there are just no boundaries on what you can achieve. Each of us has the entire quantum universe at our creative disposal - what more could we need than that? Each and every one of us has not just the ability, but the *right* to create of our own free will. Our right to create is as fundamental as our right and ability to Love, or to be in Truth. We have no *obligation* to create, no more than we are obligated to act from Love or to be in Truth. Our free will is inviolable in this. But when we are in touch with our real-self, we are aware that the only moral choice we have is to take action and to create what is right because it is right. And it is only when we create that we can ever really be fulfilled or achieve real abundance.

Perhaps you love to cook. When you lovingly prepare a meal, it is replete with Feeling, isn't it? Whoever eats your food can feel *you*, indeed they can feel your love, through the food you've prepared. While creation may touch people in the form of a masterpiece, far more often it is a simple piece of street art. For every epic oratorio, there are countless little songs that touch us in the deepest recesses of our hearts. When you consider the sheer breadth of what people turn into art – sculptures out of matchsticks, portraits out of pizza, illuminations out of packing tape, clothing out of milk – no one could possibly deny that this whole creation thing is who we are, and it's *big*. Our creativity and the creations that result are not of huge import because of our rare epic masterpieces. Our creations matter so very much because of all of those countless, seemingly insignificant creative actions taken by so very many of us. Just as with our intuition, it is our creative baby steps that really matter. Through our quantum connectedness, each of our little creations is a cascade of love that permeates the universe, and like a cascade or shower of particles from a gamma ray burst, our creations give birth to a multitude of creations we can scarcely imagine (see Figure 8.2). This is creative synergy on a truly grand scale, and this is how the universe works. This is why our creations only require a small "critical mass" of us to make an astounding difference in which reality/universe we live in. It gives you chills when you begin to feel just what our creative power is all about.

When we create, our intuition is the connection, the link, the communication pathway between our true feelings and the creations that result in the physical world. Creation devoid of feeling is no creation at all. What is called Mental "creativity" - the kind so many of us do at work - is not real creation. We "fill our belly" when we create with our true feelings using our intuition. We create when we let go and we just say "Fuck it! I'm creating this because it is the right thing to create! And I know this is the right thing to create because I can *feel* it."

Feelingization

Olympians, expert mountain climbers, freestyle athletes, and dancers all do it. You've heard it called "visualization", but this is really a misnomer. What they are describing is not about, certainly not predominantly about, developing some kind of clear mental picture in the minds eye. What these experts are really talking about is *feelingization: intuitively developing a feeling that is so complete and real it is as if the event has already happened.* Of course, the event *has* already happened, not in the athlete's or performer's current experience of 4D Physicality, but in another universe/reality, just as real and accessible to your 8D+ feeling-self. But which version or small subset of versions of the event or performance do we choose to intuit? There are a multitude of 4D realities in which the event or performance happens/happened, so many in fact that our feeble mental-self is next to useless in trying to "visualize" even a smattering of them.

Feelingization has nothing to do with developing multiple versions of a mental movie of our "future" life. There are so many variables that could occur in what we call "real" time, an athlete or performer would scarcely know which versions to visualize. Or put a bit differently, how could an athlete or performer mentally visualize all reasonable versions of their event? They can't, of course, no one could. True, their 8D+ feeling-selves easily access and understand all of these realities, but athletes and performers execute their art in the Physicality of space-time, not in Feelingality.

Enter intuition. Our intuition has no trouble dealing with what appears to be an intractable conundrum. Our intuition is designed to communicate with our feeling-self; it is the process that "steps down" 8D+ reality to 4D space-time Physicality. We don't need to know how it all works to use it, no more than we need to know exactly how an airplane operates to fly in one. We have an erroneous - a deliberately erroneous - idea that it is only Mentality which is detailed and precise, while Feelings are vague and nondescript, wishy-washy things of no particular value. It is exactly the opposite! What then do "detailed and precise" feelings feel like? Remember a very special event or place in your life. What makes that event or place or experience so indelibly etched in your being, a permanent part of who you are? Is it the bits and bytes of some kind of mental memory? Is it some precise memory of some exact set of circumstances, like some clip of a scene in a movie, that makes the memory so wonderfully powerful? Of course not. It is the *feeling* of it, coupled with all of the associated physical experiences – smells, sights, tastes, sounds - all of these are far more detailed and precise than any mental record could ever hope to be. There is *nothing* at all imprecise about these kinds of "memories", they are very real and extraordinarily complex, yet they are far easier to access and relive than recalling the amount of the last deposit into your bank account. Our true feelings prove once again to be infallible, and our intuition proves to be our infallible guide through life. Or down a ski run....

Skiing

Consider a world cup skier mentally visualizing his (so-called) future run down a steep slalom course down a 3500 meter-high mountain. He has a superb mental picture, what he calls a "visualization" of the run, the result of many hours of "seeing" his way down the run, every gate, every barrier, the sunshine hitting the course at the time of day he will make his run, even accounting for the exact sun angle projected for that day. He's reviewed many hours of film. He even thought of whether or not he should visualize the run under cloudy conditions, but for this time of year, there is a 96% chance according to weather forecasts that his run will happen on a sunny day. He tried to account for the quality of the snow in his "mental visualization", realizing that even though sunshine was all but guaranteed this time of year, the temperature indeed could vary quite a bit due to warming downslope winds, so the snow could range from powdery to sloppy slush. He tried to account for this, but his "mental visualization" failed him here, because this was a feature he could not successfully "visualize" very well even though it was a physical one. And now, the day of the run has arrived. He is scheduled to start in two hours, and after a sunny beginning to the day, the weather has become raw, damp, and completely overcast. One hour before his run, a freezing drizzle begins to fall, and by the time of his run, a hard coating of ice has formed up at the top of the mountain. But the reports from the lower part of the run are even worse: conditions have indeed turned to slush. Our skier begins his run, unnerved but still confident in his "visualization" training, for he and his coach covered a variety of weather scenarios in their mental "visualizations" in which they "conquered this mountain". But the combination of all of the things happening simultaneously this afternoon were not quite one of them. Things go pretty well in the upper part of his run, and the snow conditions here were indeed one of his "visualized scenarios", but the weather and visibility ahead were not. Our skier realizes it is not the bottom of the run he sees ahead, but a dense bank of ground fog, only halfway down the mountain. He loses almost all visual cues as he enters the fog bank, sensory overload sets in, and within seconds our skier misses what should have been one of the easier gates on the entire hill. The rest of his trip down the mountain is uneventful, he doesn't even notice the slush at the bottom of the mountain, because the competition is over for him and he scores a DNF. But our skier makes one firm resolution to himself as he crosses the finish: it is indeed time to find a new coach.

Now let's consider a world cup skier *"feelingizing"* her way down the same slope as her unfortunate male "predecessor" (actually he did the run on the exact same date and time, and with exactly the same conditions, but in an otherwise alternate universe from the one where our skier is doing her run). She has studied not just the same *kind* of data, but actually the *same data* as the male skier. But her preparations went beyond his: she felt, *truly felt* every bit of the way down the mountain in her "feelingization" practice with her coach, every bump, every nuance of the surface. She didn't just feel the run, but she felt the living consciousness of the mountain itself (she would have called it kami, if she knew the term); this was something she always practiced in her "feelingization". She spoke to very few people about feeling the very consciousness of a mountain, not so much because she worried people would think she was weird, for she embraced weird, but because if she did talk about this, people would think she was being cute, or metaphorical, when she was being neither. Her preparations went even further, however, and this was not something she was consciously aware of yet in this part of her life: she was not just feeling hypothetical runs down the mountain whose wave functions never collapsed into 4D, but she was also feeling the countless runs down the mountain which were true feelings of runs down the mountain in other realities, runs "already" manifested in 4D but still in her "future" as far as her wristwatch could tell. (Each of these runs were manifestations of alternate universes whose wave functions had "already" collapsed with certainty. We'll explore what this means in Chapter 7, Quantum). Well, even if she heard of these arcane physics terms, she never would have mentally understood what they meant, and in any case, even if she did mentally understand the physics it would have been useless in helping her get down the mountain. Far more importantly, her 8D+ self *felt* every detail of all of these "past", "present" and "future" feelings of the slalom run, just as she *felt* the kami of the mountain. She used her intuition to process all of these feelings in 4D physicality. When she made her run, under the exact meteorological conditions we described before, she hit the cloud/fog bank, lost her visual cues, and had no *idea* what to do ... but she *felt* exactly what she must do, she skied every gate perfectly, and completed the course in world record time. When asked by an interviewer shortly after crossing the finish line, she told him she *felt* she could ski this mountain blindfolded. He thought this was hyperbole, but of course she knew it wasn't.

There is one short postscript to this story: our male skier was actually a very sensitive soul. He was a very good, sometimes exceptional skier who always told anyone who would listen that he skied not to win, and not for sponsorships or money or free gear and clothing, but because he just loved the mountains. He became a truly great skier, after he fired his coach and hired the same coach as our female skier. She would be his coach for the rest of his life.

Chapter 6

Gaia

Wind-time, wolf-time, ere the world falls ...

Yggdrasil shakes

and shiver on high the ancient limbs

and the giant is loose

- Völuspá,[1] Stanzas 45, 47

There are two threads weaving deeply through the narrative of earth. One is the human thread, the other is the thread of Gaia. It is a far better world when both threads are woven in synchrony and harmony, but such is not the state of our planet. Earth has been discordant for quite some time now. Both threads have become tattered and frayed, and the weave is very wrong.

Consider a housefly. Have you ever wondered why it is so difficult to swat one with your hand, let alone to manually catch one? Or think of trying to catch a squirrel with your bare hands. A pretty impossible task for you, or even for your cat or dog. There is a clear and probably astonishing scientific explanation. It turns out time itself - more accurately, clock time - runs much slower for houseflies and squirrels. Like the character Neo in *The Matrix* evading bullets, to the fly or the squirrel, your motion is comically slow. The fly can finish reading her newspaper before she has to bother evading what you perceive as your hand speeding toward her. It is much the same for the squirrel, who is laughing high up the tree before you, your cat, or your dog have gotten anywhere near the tree trunk.[2,3]

Plants. They smell, they see, they communicate, they behave altruistically,[4] insects use them to "leave voice mail", and they can integrate more diverse information than any animal. Plants smell using incredibly minute traces of pheromones that would put any animal's sense of smell to shame.[5] Plants see by seeing colors, and light intensities, and thus directions of light.[6] Plants communicate not just between their roots, but above ground, too. They don't just evaluate the locations of food, or their competition, thus making decisions based on their environment,[7] but they assess the location and condition of their relatives, altruistically helping members of their family to grow and develop without any benefit to themselves.[8] Plants solve the "risk versus reward" dilemma as well as any animal, and far better than any capitalist. And insects use plants to leave "voice mail" messages for other insects by changing the chemical composition of plant leaves, thus leaving messages for those (of the same or even other species!) who show up in the future.[9]

We may be tempted to ask "can plants think as well as animals do?" but should we instead be asking "do animals, think, or reason, as well as plants?" Or for that matter, "do humans think at all?" From building nuclear plants in seismic zones (France, not just Japan),[10] to toxic fracking in the Canadian Northwest, in one of the last remaining pristine regions of earth (consequently poisoning the First Nations people who live there),[11] from the systematic murder of gorillas[12] to the genocide of whales and dolphins,[13] the human repertoire of exploitation, destruction and death is unmatched and frightening to behold. Humans destroy their own food supply through anthropogenic global warming and desertification. We damage it further with genetically modified (GMO) crops, simply for the base reasons of profit and keeping the 3rd world subjugated. We then finish things off by poisoning our food supply with agricultural chemicals. in 1940, there were almost no pesticides or herbicides used worldwide, and about 3.5% of the harvest was lost to insects and weeds. We now apply 1000 times more pesticides and herbicides per unit area of agricultural land than we did in 1940, and the result: *12% of the harvest is now lost* to pests and weeds.[14]

And yet, astoundingly, and despite us, there is so much that *still* functions on earth, and functions remarkably well. The incredibly complex, integrated consciousness that is Gaia is running superbly despite our negligence and outright attacks on Her. In this book it has proved unavoidable to highlight the discouraging – not to have done so would be denying the reality, gravity, and immediacy of our plight. Even on the brink of destruction as we are, Gaia, and *all* of her creatures, continue to give us so much hope, even as they hold their collective breaths to see what we will do, or what we will choose not to do. And our time is very, very short. We have neither millennia nor centuries to get our act together, at best we have only decades. Gaia is here to support us, to provide for all of our needs, and to be our loving partner no matter how terribly we treat Her (one more confirmation that Gaia is indeed Feminine). We must really start listening to Her by listening to our own intuition, and we must begin treating Her with the same kind of love and respect with which She unquestioningly treats us. When we appreciate Her unparalleled beauty even a tiny bit, when we show Her even in very small ways that we do love Her, when we just attempt to commune with Her, we will be astounded by how much She gives us in return. After all, what mother wouldn't?

Hi, Gaia!

We spend our entire lives here, we are dependent on this system for our very existence, and yet many of us barely know Gaia. What, or rather who, is She?

- *Gaia is the consciousness of earth.*
- *Gaia is the consciousness of **all** of the life that comprises earth.*
- *Gaia is a wholly integrated system of life and consciousness.*
- *Gaia is Herself a living organism.*

The earth corresponds to your Physical-self, whereas Gaia corresponds to your Feeling-self. So Gaia and earth are the same in the sense that your Feeling-self and Physical-self constitute the same you. Thus Gaia's *consciousness* has nothing to do with Mentality or mental constructs, but belongs to the realm of Feeling. *Life* includes the *entirety* of the earth system, and is not limited to 4D space-time. In addition to what we usually consider biological life, such as plants, animals, fungi, and bacteria, life includes rocks and minerals and soil, the oceans and all bodies of water, even the atmosphere itself. Therefore, the consciousness of earth, that is Gaia, includes the consciousnesses of not just biological life, but the rocks and minerals and soil, oceans and bodies of water and the atmosphere, too. Am I suggesting that rocks, the oceans, the atmosphere and all the rest have *actual* consciousness? I'm not only suggesting this, I'm stating it as fact. We may not notice the consciousness of a rock for just the same reason that we are barely noticeable to a housefly. The speed of clock time for a rock runs much, much slower than it does for us, the "data rate" of that rock's consciousness is much slower than ours, but its consciousness is nonetheless just as real as that of any plant or animal, human or otherwise.

And there is even more to life. Earth's life, and thus her consciousness, also includes **supra-dimensional beings** that inhabit dimensions "higher" than 4D Physicality (some of them span from 4D into adjacent "higher" dimensions). Who are these supra-dimensional beings? They are known by innumerable names; European usage includes faeries, nymphs, nereids, naiads, dryads, sprites, elves, elementals, gnomes, trolls,[15] huldufólk,[16] and all manner of little and not-so-little "people" dwelling at the edges of human mental consciousness and beyond. How do we "see" these beings or interact with them? We can't ordinarily see them, but we can definitely sense them and interact with them using our intuition, augmented by our physical senses.

As a living, integrated system of life and consciousness, Gaia has a crucially important **immune system** which keeps Her in balance. Gaia's immune system is autonomic, extraordinarily powerful, and always impacts all of life on earth. When Gaia is under attack, however - which means, of course, now - Gaia's immune system must kick into very high gear and Her immune system affects us far more than anyone would like it to be. Nonetheless, like the immune system of any organism, Gaia's automatic immune response is crucial to the survival of the Gaia super-organism. Gaia's immune system has been more active in the past 150 years than She needed it to be in the prior 15,000 years, and Her immune system has been far more active in the past 5 years than She needed it to be in the previous 150 years.

Does Gaia Herself have **free will**? Do the manifold creatures with kami have free will? If by free will it is meant that through their kami they could choose to ignore the system of Gaia, or to harm Gaia in any way, the answer is definitively no, the kami could never do this. None of Gaia's creatures with kami could ever exercise any kind of destructive free will. Likewise, supra-dimensional beings have latitude in their consciousness resembling the free will of humans, but supra-dimensional beings can never exercise their free will against Gaia, either. It would not make any sense for them to do so, since the avowed role of supra-dimensional beings is to protect and support Gaia. The only creatures who can exercise their free will for good or ill are the few individuated animal species.

The Kami and Individuated Animals

There is however another very special category of consciousness, integral with and essential to the existence of the Gaia system Herself. These are the **kami**. The kami are not life in the same sense as animals or plants or even rocks or water, but they are very much alive as consciousness. Kami are the collective consciousnesses of almost all of our planet's myriad life forms (humans and cetaceans, for example, do not have kami; we will discuss this shortly). We can neither physically see kami, nor can we mentally or physically "talk" to them, but we can very much sense them and they us, they "hear" us and interact with and indeed converse with us in the realm of Feeling, via our intuition.

I use the Shinto term kami for these consciousnesses, these "nature spirits" of earth's myriad life forms, because kami is a far better and more accurate term than any other I've encountered. For one thing, the notion of kami is so integrated with and essential to Shinto belief that no other readily accessible philosophical system comes close to accurately characterizing them, or just how ubiquitous and essential the kami are (although by a tendency to anthropomorphize them, even modern Shinto practice does not render them very accurately). The term kami is also accurate because it cannot be defined semantically or mentally comprehended; kami can only be sensed, intuited, and felt. (Shinto practitioners say if you have to define kami in order to understand who they are, then you do not understand kami). Nowadays only a very few humans seek out or interact with kami, let alone communicate with and embrace them, while a large majority of humans ignore them completely. (Given their Shinto tradition and practices one would hope most Japanese would know better, but the abysmal Japanese environmental record belies that expectation). We'll try to get to know kami better here, even though they truly must be felt via our intuition to be known, and human language constructs are completely inadequate in accurately describing them. Kami are everywhere, and along with all life on the planet we humans are affected by kami, always, no matter how urban our environment may be.

The bonds among kami are the bonds of sisters.
The bonds between Gaia and Her kami
are the bonds of a loving Mother with her daughters.

At the discrete level, there are kami associated with what we perceive as solitary life forms, such as the kami of a particular daisy flower, or granite rock, or hedgehog, or pine tree. These kami function as an extension of the consciousness of that daisy or granite or hedgehog or tree, and have a vital role in connecting the consciousness of a particular life form with the kami of other life forms, and hence with the consciousnesses of those other life forms. The rock's, daisy's, hedgehog's, or pine tree's kami connect with related life forms, which can be one of two kinds:

(1) those life forms who are spatially related (geographically proximate, or in the same ecosystem), and

(2) life forms of the same species who may be geographically distant or who dwell in a distant ecosystem.[1]

Let's assume the hedgehog, daisy, and granite all live in your garden, so they are geographically close and belong to the same ecosystem. The pine tree – a baby pine tree – lives in a small wood adjoining your garden. Each has its own kami, but how do these kami communicate? Not only are these life forms quite different, but their "clocks" run at very different rates (from a human "clock" perspective, granite's clock runs extremely slowly, the baby pine tree's still quite slow, but the hedgehog's clock is quite fast compared to ours). From the perspective of human mentality, it makes no sense that these life forms with vastly different clock speeds could interact with each other at all. For the kami, however, these differences in clock speeds present no problems whatsoever.

The connections between and among kami are not in 4D Physicality, but in the 8D+ realm of Feelingality. Thus they are not bound by any strictures of clock time, for clock time itself is meaningless in 8D+. Not only is feeling-based communication instantaneous, but it doesn't matter if it spans the distance of your garden, halfway around the planet, or across the universe.

---

[1] The term "species" in terms of kami is similar to the use of the term species in cladistics, rather than as it is used in classical Linnaean taxonomy.

In this way the kami of your garden have no difficulty communicating with their fellow kami of the same species across Gaia, regardless of geographic distance. The kami of your garden daisy communicate just as facilely and accurately with the kami of the other daisies in your garden, as they do with the daisies in your neighbors garden, or with the kami of a patch of daisies dwelling in a distant alpine meadow.

There is another kind of kami, a type of overarching kami, who encompass all of a species in an area, a region, or even globally. So there is a kami for all of the granite rock in your neighborhood, and a kami for the granite rock in your region, a kami for all of the granite rock on earth, an overarching kami for all of the granite in the solar system, the galaxy, and so on. Likewise there is a kami for your friendly garden hedgehog, as well as a kami for all of the hedgehogs flung across the world. There is a kami for an individual pine tree, an overarching kami for a stand of pine trees, and an overarching kami for all of the pine trees worldwide. There are overarching kami of the atmosphere and of the oceans, as well kami for the different oceanic and atmospheric layers, just as there are kami of specific oceanic regions, bays, fjords, watercourses, and lakes. The kami of oceanic and atmospheric currents are naturally fluid and in constant motion, making it particularly difficult for humans to envision or relate to them, yet of all the kami, these have the greatest direct and immediate impact on humans and human society. None of this will be surprising or unfamiliar to the indigenous reader, and it would have not been alien to pre-Christian Europeans, either. The former would have much to teach us about Gaia and Her kami, if we would only listen to them, and the latter are an audience that doesn't seem to be here anymore.

What are the purposes of kami communications? For the kami of an individual life form or species, like our daisy or hedgehog, their primary role is to nurture and protect the life form for whom they are responsible, and their interactions with other kami of other life forms is primarily to ensure "their" life form is nurtured and protected. First and foremost, then, these kami zealously do all they can to care for "their" life form. Next, they interact with the kami of neighboring life forms, i.e. those life forms geographically nearby or part of the same ecosystem, but who are not the same or a closely related species. There are kami of that local ecosystem, say your back garden, or a small nearby pond, and they just as zealously do all they can to nurture and protect their ecosystem. (If only highway and construction engineers would acknowledge this everywhere as they do in Iceland, there would be much less adverse environmental impact in highway construction projects). Overarching kami naturally focus on the nurture and protection of their area, region, or even planet-wide. Kami interactions, from the perspective of the kami, are interactions in Feelingality, and hence are simple and supremely logical among the kami. These same kami interactions can make sense to us, too, when we apply our intuition to listen to them. But as soon as we try to understand or communicate with kami at the level of Mentality, our understanding evaporates and our communications become impossible, just like the hopeless attempts at mental visualization made by our skier in Chapter 5, or the Dyads' efforts to mentally understand the concept of 3D. The kami also interact and coordinate with the supra-dimensional beings in doing their work (e.g. the fairy of a daisy, the elf of a granite rock, or the nereid of an ocean bay). When there are, for example, two or more life forms requiring the same resource in a given ecosystem, the interacting kami do their best to meet the needs of all affected life forms in the ecosystem, and they minimize any negative impact to other life forms as much as possible. Far too often, however, human environmental negligence and destruction puts enormous pressure on kami and they are faced with dreadful dilemmas and Hobsonian choices which no kami should ever have to face. These kami weep when they have to make choices about saving one life form at the expense of other ones.

Using our intuition, we can and should strive to actively communicate with the kami by *feeling* them, just as we should strive to use our intuition to communicate with our own true feeling-selves. It is no accident that we have a favorite flower we tend, a special rock upon which we sit, a beach we find particularly relaxing, or a tree whose boughs we just can't resist sitting beneath. This is us tuning into kami who particularly resonate with us (more often it is the kami initiating communication with us, than it is us initiating with them). We must seize these opportunities to communicate with the more extrovert kami - many kami are quite shy - to hone our abilities to communicate with many other kami. We can use the same methodology to communicate with supra-dimensional beings, in fact communicating with many of them is more akin to human communication because many of their consciousnesses extend down to 4D space-time.

Consider how weather profoundly affects us. It is no accident that there are rainy, stormy days that invigorate us and bring us joy, and other similarly rainy and stormy days which depress and unnerve us. This is true for sunny days, too. There are sunny days we find joyous and exhilarating, but perhaps surprisingly, there are those sunny days that we can't help but feeling melancholy. This is us tuning into the kami of the atmosphere; all of the kami want us to tune into and connect with them. Like us, kami have moods, though they would much prefer being happy all of the time. The kami *need* us to communicate with them, to hear them, to feel what they are feeling, and to have an active, sincere dialog with them. The kami need our help, and nowadays, they *desperately* need our help. The kami are overjoyed, and send messages of joy to their respective life forms, when we *do* connect with them and help even in the seemingly smallest ways. Tending your daisies, creating a friendly environment for your hedgehogs (never give them milk!), respecting your granite rocks, or stepping off the path and saying "hi!" to the baby pine tree, each of these little acts are just as loved and appreciated by the kami as stopping pesticide and herbicide use, preventing a fracking well or an offshore oil well, or harnessing the power of the sun, wind, tides and currents to meet our electrical needs. The kami appreciate it when we do big things, but they are ecstatic when any of us take baby steps to join them.

Individuated Animals

A small but important group of animals do not have kami at all, but they do have Mentality and with it the ability to exercise complete free will, i.e. the free will to do good, or harm, to Gaia and her creatures. These **individuated animals** include, in descending order of necessity to the survival and health of the Gaia system, and thus in descending order of intelligence:

- cetaceans
- birds (some)[§]
- wolves
- elephants
- cats
- non-human primates
- humans

[§] Birds constitute a special category. They are individuated by nature, but many species can and do choose to live in flocks through a purely democratic voting process. In a flock, birds create and adhere to a collective flock-consciousness that behaves very much like a flock "kami", but individuals are always free to break away from the flock (occasionally they are cast out due to poor behavior). All of this may sound really far-fetched, except to ornithologists, who continue to be astounded by the advanced level of bird intelligence, communication abilities, and social structures. Some birds, such as parrots, crows, doves and pigeons, are truly individuated, whereas others, like domestic fowl and starlings, are not. Bird individuation covers a wide spectrum.

These animals are called "individuated" because they have completely individuated their consciousnesses and now make individual decisions (though all of these species had kami in the distant past). Being individuated means these species are completely responsible for the moral, or immoral, decisions they make, and they can choose to help, or to harm. Notably, only humans and a few primate species ever make the choice to deliberately harm. While some primates do harm one another in a very human-like way, humans have the distinction of being the only animal who chooses to harm and attack the planet and Gaia Herself. We humans may be important to our planet's survival, but cetaceans are crucial. Earth Herself would perish without cetaceans, just as earth's oceans would perish without sharks. Among the individuated animals, humans are the least important for Gaia's ultimate survival, but we hold the potential to be exceptionally powerful in helping and nurturing Gaia back to health. At a minimum, we humans have an obligation to do all we can possibly do to right the egregious wrongs we have inflicted on our home planet and Her life.

When humans harm other individuated animals, including of course other humans, this is an egregious violation of Gaia which disturbs the entire planet. When humans harm entities with kami, their actions can be dismissed at times due to ignorance, but no such dismissal is possible when we bring harm to other individuated animals. When humans deliberately kill any individuated animal, whether that animal is a fellow human, cetacean, wolf, elephant, cat, or primate, this is murder.

When we humans willingly destroy a population of these animals, this is genocide. When the crew of a Sea Shepherd mission affirm that they are willing to put their own lives on the line to save the life of a whale or dolphin, this is no different than their saying they will put their lives on the line to protect a fellow human. This is sadly just what humans like Joy and George Adamson, Dian Fossey, and Ymke Warren were called to do in the protection of our fellow individuated animals. There is no getting around it when it comes to individuated animals: murder is murder and genocide is genocide, and the moral ramifications of these acts are just as severe whether that individuated animal is human, or not.

Entities with kami can never be out-of-tune or out-of-synch with Gaia; they do not have the free will to be able to get out-of-tune or out-of-synch. Among those mammals with kami, there are those like raccoons or seals who are quite intelligent and fairly close to being individuated, but they still have kami to guide and advise them. On the other hand, the squirrels, skunks, groundhogs, and hedgehogs who may traffic through your garden are still very much integrated with their kami. These mammals have a kind of free will in that they can consciously choose among alternatives as to how they act, but they can never act in any way that could injure Gaia. For these kinds of mammals, their kami's feelings, which are always true feelings, guide their decisions in Physicality. The mentality they do have is completely automatic, merely implementing their feelings in physicality. Many insects, like bees and ants and termites, are almost completely guided by their kami, which for them functions as a master consciousness, making the hive or the colony a type of super-organism. When you eat vegetables, their kami plead with us to not eat genetically modified (GMO) food, warning us that we are only beginning to grasp its dangers to the planet and the risk such genetically modified food poses to the human species (much like the very present risk already posed by the use of animal antibiotics to any human themselves in need of antibiotics).[17]

There are kami of domestic animals, too, and they are gravely concerned about the plight of so many of these animals when they are subjected to the unspeakable horrors of factory farms. If you do eat the meat of domestic animals, their kami beg you to only eat animals raised in free and open conditions and slaughtered humanely. As with all life forms who in supreme acts of love give themselves up for our sustenance, it is so very important that we are thankful to these plants and animals for what they do for us. When we truly feel this thanks, the kami feel it too, and they transmit that thanks to those animals and plants we consume. It is no problem that this thanks is seemingly "backward in time" since it is in the realm of feeling which exists outside of 4D time restrictions. This indeed means that the very animals or vegetables we consume are the ones who feel our thanks via their kami, even though they are already "dead" from our 4D-time perspective. Such is the quantum way in which Feelingality works.

What's next?

Kami are not overlords in any way, but collectively they are kind of a unified super-consciousness of the entities for whom they are kami (creatures with kami could no more have kami who are overlords than they could be overlords themselves). This is why entities who have kami do not have free will like that of individuated animals, but through their kami they have a collective will, and that collective will is by definition tuned into and synchronized with Gaia.

Are there really "good kami" and "bad kami"? No, but kami can certainly be in good or bad moods, depending on the conditions faced by their life forms. By now it should be obvious to anyone that when they attack earth's life, ecosystems, or indeed the entire planet as we do with human-caused global warming, that does not put the kami in a good mood, and unhappy kami make for an unhappy, unstable planet. The kami of the atmosphere and of the oceans react with enormous impact, as do the kami of the Greenland and Antarctic ice sheets, for example. The moods of the kami are quite important, and have a great impact on what happens on our planet, because the kami are so very passionate and loyal about defending and protecting their Gaia. The kami mean no harm in any of their reactions and responses to the dreadful things humans do; they are simply playing their role in Gaia's immune system, doing what it must do to protect itself. Unfortunately – and this bears all of the hallmarks of patriarchy – it is often the humans who are the poorest and most downtrodden, and those with the least deleterious impact on Gaia, who suffer the most as Gaia's immune system ramps up on the planet. The kami would far prefer to work with us – and they are overjoyed when we *do* work with them! – but just as they will do all they can to defend and protect their life forms, they will also do their utmost to protect Gaia via her immune system, whatever the cost to humans must be.

The actions of kami can and do manifest as a tsunami on a clear day, an unpredicted earthquake, the eruption of a long-dormant volcano, or a devastating drought, just as much as rapidly rising sea levels, melting glaciers, or crumbling mountains, but the actions of kami can and do manifest as a beautiful day at the beach, a stand of scrub pines that smell amazingly fresh and make you giddy, animal traffic in your garden or squirrels knocking at your door, or a gentle steady rain or comforting breeze that comes just when it's needed. We know which of these kami reactions *feel* right, and we should just as automatically realize which ones are telling us that something is terribly wrong. Yet somehow we readily appreciate the latter, and wantonly disregard the former.

The die off of bees and amphibians worldwide is not just a warning sign of an environment on the edge of catastrophe, these are portents of imminent cataclysm. If we take heed, and take heed now, it is still not too late for happy kami to rule the day. Not only would that be wonderful for all of us, but the survival of the human species depends upon it.

Gaia really is very, very forgiving, but eventually a point is reached where She can sustain no more and things must boil over. This is when extremes become the norm, and extremes are not a good thing. If it were possible to direct Gaia's immune reaction specifically back to those who perpetrate it, Gaia would certainly do that, but Gaia is an immense organism, much like a biological cell. When a cell is under attack and fights an infection, it fights with all its effort, and in a real crisis it cannot fight selectively. Such too is the case with Gaia. This unfortunately means that the good and innocent fall victim along with the evil and responsible. It was no coincidence, for example, that the Lisbon tsunami and fire of 1755 followed genocides in the New World. About 20,000 dolphins were murdered in an annual genocide on the east coast of Japan until a few years ago. The earthquake and ensuing tsunami of 2011, however, destroyed much of the infrastructure used to hunt the dolphins (except in the Taiji cove itself), thus saving as many as 18,000 dolphins per year since the tsunami. In 2013 the unprecedented and immensely powerful typhoon Haiyan devastated major portions of the Philippines and southeast Asia killing an estimated 10,000 people and leaving 11,000,000 people homeless or displaced. These events are not any kind of retribution – Gaia would never do that to any of Her creatures, not even humans, and this is not how the universe works, but these events are the result of the reactions of Gaia's immune system to the brutality Her creatures have suffered. When the kami are unhappy and depressed due to the dreadful behavior of men, then the destruction and destabilization caused by these men must be corrected and re-stabilized. Sadly, the suffering caused by Gaia's immune response disproportionately affects the innocent and downtrodden in places like Bangladesh or the Philippines or Indonesia, adding to the miserable consequences of patriarchal feudal capitalism. The innocent perish in the flood while the culpable escape to higher ground.

The evidence is overwhelming and it is everywhere: the kami are on the move and Gaia's immune system is kicking into high gear, re-stabilizing, re-harmonizing, and re-synchronizing Gaia so that She can be healed and restored to the brilliant emanation of Goddess which She is meant to be. Gaia and her kami along with all of the individuated animals of earth (with the notable exception of us humans) are not bent on destruction, they are all about love and healing and bringing things back into balance. Many of them have suffered profoundly at the hands of the human species, yet still they wait with steadfast patience, hoping against hope that we finally "get it" and will change our ways, even at this latest of hours, but the breaking points are being reached, and they are being breached. There *is* no counter-argument to feeling Gaia, to feeling and sensing and heeding the cries of Her creatures and all of their kami. Despite all of the love emanating from all of the life forms that comprise the system that is Gaia, the defense mechanisms of Gaia's immune system must engage, and they are engaging. Gaia will do all that she can to preserve her children. This has never before meant turning on one of Her own species in a kind of autoimmune response for the benefit of all the rest, but that is just the precipice on which we find ourselves. Gaia and all of Her life and all of the kami too will weep if humans disappear from the earth. They would all far prefer we get our act together, but if saving all of Her non-human life forms necessitates an earth without us, that will happen, and it will happen quite soon. The upheaval and pain caused by our disappearance from the earth would be immense, but Gaia will survive, and once again thrive. It is solely up to us whether we'll be here or not.

Why even worry about the presence of humans at all? Why indeed? Wouldn't the earth simply be better without them? Despite the power of all of the Goddess-centric individuated creatures of the earth, the elephants and dolphins and whales and wolves and cats and primates of so many kinds, despite myriad kami and uncountable supra-dimensional creatures ... it is humans, and *only* humans, who can easily reverse the path to destruction that these same humans have set the earth on. In a sense, by acceding to and accepting patriarchal control, most of humanity are holding the earth hostage, and this will be the unfortunate reality for a short while more. You see that it is inconsequential whether or not patriarchy rules the earth actively, or via our tacit acquiescence? For Gaia and the planet, the result is the same. The good news is we are getting very close to the point in 4D-time where humans will have either reversed their course toward utter destruction and demonstrably turned themselves toward Truth, Love, Gaia and Goddess, or they will have sealed their demise. The natural processes of Gaia crying out for Her children and Her immune system responding have been particularly felt over the past decade. This is just an acrid foretaste of what is going to follow if we remain on this destructive non-path.

Probabilities

It is with reluctance that I include the next section of this chapter, but I realize omitting it would be withholding information that my own intuition keeps telling me I must include. Please keep in mind that probabilities are just that, probabilities, they are not certainties, and be careful not to misunderstand what this means.[§] The potential for planetary wake-up calls by wildfires, volcanism, extreme storms, earthquakes, tsunamis, drought, desertification and flooding is far from having reached any kind of peak. Some humans are awakening to these present realities and are at least considering doing something about it, but the time for considering is long past. If even after these planetary wake-up calls, humans still do not change their course, the earth will have no choice but to do all She can to cleanse Herself of us. We don't want to be here for that. Any survival of humanity would be a restart, reliant on

---

[§] for example, if the probability of an event occurring in any given year is 1-in-100, say a "hundred year flood", that does *not* mean the probability of it happening in the next ten years is 10-in-100; the probability remains 1-in-100 for each year over the next 10 years.

humans surviving off planet and then, if allowed, to begin repopulating earth. So here's one thing the patriarchy's preposterous "bible" actually got right: no human will want to be alive if these times happen. But unlike the predictions in their so-called "bible", there is no certainty that these cataclysmic events will happen.

It does seem, though, that as a species we've hit the snooze button on some kind of cataclysmic alarm clock. Will we wake up this time, when the alarm must ring even more shrilly? Preliminary indications are not so good – UN climate conferences that promise almost nothing and achieve even less, hopeful change like the Energiewende in Germany vowing the end of nuclear power, but instead disastrously ramping up brown coal production, the US and China and India doing, well, nothing ... patriarchal power systems remain entrenched, and the kind of real change the planet needs remains far from our grasp. It's not clear just how close humanity is to the "midnight hour" of their destruction, but it seems we must get even closer to that point to do anything meaningful to reverse the terrible things we've done for patriarchy. The next 2 years will likely see a doubling of wake-up calls, and the subsequent 15 years will see a geometric increase in these wake-up calls if there is no substantive real change. After that, from about 2031 onward, if humanity has still not changed their course, "all bets are off". So really, that seems to be our window – 20 or 30 years at most from 2014 – for us to implement real, substantive change. Otherwise, we seriously risk extinction, because mechanisms in Gaia's immune system will have been launched which we can no longer stop in time to save us. It will simply be too late.

If humanity remains on their course of destruction, the period 2031 to 2048 will be dreadful. On this stupid and perhaps still reversible course, by 2054 at least 95% of humans will be under severe survival pressure. By 2066, over 99% of humans will be devastated, struggling for survival, in war or in famine, desperate for clean water, fruitful soil, and breathable air. It would very much be "back to the beginning" for those who survive, just as it was for early modern humans in the East African rift valley so many years ago. At that point, it would be equally likely that humans will be wiped out completely as not, and it is unlikely that those humans who would have survived by leaving the earth would be allowed to re-colonize anyway. In these scenarios, humans needn't concern themselves with asteroid impacts post-2070; they won't be around to experience them anyway.

Table 6.2 lists estimated probabilities, as of early 2014, of the occurrence of some (certainly not all) potentially cataclysmic events.

The significance of these probability ranges are categorized in Table 6.1:

Probability	Category
0.01 *to* 0.03	Significant
0.04 *to* 0.08	Serious
0.09 *to* 0.12	Major
0.13 *to* 0.24	Dangerous
> 0.25	Grave

Table 6.1 - Severity Classes of Cataclysmic Events by Probability

The following table (6.2) lists the probability of an event occurring over a specific range of years. For example, there is a probability of 0.04, i.e. a probability of 4%, or said differently a 4-in-100 chance, of a major Icelandic volcano outbreak occurring in any of the years 2014 through 2017. This may not sound very high, but consider rolling a die, and the likelihood of an even number occurring in any one of three rolls of that die. The probability of seeing a 2, 4, or 6 in one of the next three rolls of that die is *not* 50% as one might think, it is actually 0.875 (87.5%). In fact the probability of *not* seeing an even number in one of those three rolls is only 0.125 (12.5%). So if, for example, we are faced with a probability of 0.4 (40%) of Beijing becoming an uninhabitable desert by any given year in the 2023 through 2031 timeframe, the probability of that event happening sometime in that period of years is very high indeed. The probabilities in this table are "worst case", but far too often, the worst case does happen.

Table 6.2 - Probability Estimates of Some Cataclysmic Events

Event/ YearRange	2014~ 2017	2017~ 2023	2023~ 2031	2031~ 2048	2049~ 2070
Yellowstone caldera, massive eruption	0.001 (0.1% probability)	0.020 (2% probability)	0.080	0.15 (15% probability)	0.470
Icelandic volcano outbreak, major	0.040	0.160	0.320	0.640	0.920
North Atlantic tsunami, massive, impacting North American east coast	0.010	0.040	0.160	0.320	0.500
North Atlantic tsunami, impacting European southwest and west coast, British Isles and Ireland	0.010	0.030	0.180	0.360	0.640
Mt. Rainer, massive eruption	0.020	0.070	0.320	0.780	0.990
0.5 km diameter asteroid impact, massive destruction	<0.001	0.004	0.030	0.120	0.240

Event/ Year Range	2014~ 2017	2017~ 2023	2023~ 2031	2031~ 2048	2049~ 2070
Desertification of Beijing (desert reaches Beijing)	0.001 *(0.1% probability)*	0.040 *(4% probability)*	0.400	0.990	>0.99
Mega-storm in California, or Western Europe, or British Isles, massive loss of life and property	0.040	0.140	0.640	0.880	0.920
Massive Pacific Rim earthquake, major loss of life in US from earthquake and ensuing tsunami	0.050	0.120	0.260	0.480	0.640
Death of 98% all sharks	0.001	0.010	0.080	0.180	0.880
Death of all the oceans	<0.001	<0.001	0.020	0.040	0.180
Massive famine (> 1 billion people) due to extreme rainfall and/or drought	0.040	0.090	0.160	0.470	0.920
Death of 98% of projected human population	<0.001	<0.001	0.020	0.160	0.460

Who could blame Gaia and Her kami and all of Her sisters and children for allowing all of this to proceed, that is to say, for allowing Gaia's natural immune system to function as it must? How long can we keep asking Gaia to suppress Her immune system and wait for us, all the time bringing the extinction of the oceans' sharks, indeed the death of the oceans themselves, that much nearer? How long can we expect Gaia's patience while Her whales and dolphins are murdered? Or yet another species of big cat is lost forever? Can Gaia really be expected to suffer the next elephant or gorilla genocide? Should Gaia risk Her earth being condemned to a Mars-like or Venus-like future? Of course not. No one but a patriarch or their minions could truly want any of these things to happen, and Gaia and humans who feel and love and the kami and all of the other individuated animals will ensure that none of this ever happens.

Gaia will do all in Her power to stop the worst case course of events from ever taking place, and if that means destroying humanity, that is more than likely what will happen. *Humans are deeply valuable to Gaia and to the universe, but not utterly so.* The Goddess' children will survive and thrive with or without them. We can and must do all we can to educate people about all of these things, but we can never force them to be convinced. Humans are individuated animals, and as such only their own free will can bring them to change. By educating, we assuredly are taking action. We are not in any way responsible for what anyone else does with knowledge, we are only responsible for what we choose to do, and then *do*, or choose not to do, and then we don't do. But we can take comfort – and caution - in knowing that what we learn we cannot unlearn, and that we are imparting knowledge that cannot be unknown. Each and every human is a creator of the highest power, and our education brings us to a most liberating place: we either exercise our free will for good, or we don't. Our choice is that simple.

Eventually, the balance will be tipped in favor of the revolution, and there will be a critical mass of revolutionaries who say "no more!" and put an end to this patriarchal madness, but the big question is, will this revolution happen in time? We can count on Gaia's immune system reacting more and more from year to year until we substantively begin reversing things. Let's never forget what a subtle yet immensely powerful "weapon" we have at our disposal in fighting patriarchy and their minions, and more importantly in righting the wrongs with which they have savaged Gaia. This "weapon" is the way the universe itself operates through quantum interconnectedness. This is why it is so essential that we take those baby steps whenever we can, why we do something, however small it may seem, to help Gaia in any little way we can.

Not using a disposable coffee cup, taking a few steps off the path to pick up a piece or two of litter, reusing, repurposing,[1] and at the very least, recycling, or best of all reducing our environmental footprint in the first place by giving and sharing,

---

[1] fyi old cotton sheets and pajamas make great handkerchiefs. Think of all the plants and energy we save by this little action alone.

all of these seemingly little actions are *just* as important to Gaia and Her kami as any major international actions we take collectively. It is best to walk or ride your bicycle, but taking public transportation is still far better than driving a car (driving an environmentally destructive monstrosity idling away in traffic is criminally negligent). Every little thing we do launches a cascade of change throughout the earth, it gives the kami that much more energy to devote to environmental cleansing and positive change, it restores that much more vibrancy to the lives of the supra-dimensional beings so they can fill their role assisting Gaia's life forms, and being in service to those life forms' kami. We should not become discouraged, as difficult as that is.

The tsunami of the revolution *will* happen, it is inevitable. It is our fervent hope, all of us who comprise the Feminine, all of Gaia, all who are of Goddess, that the revolution happens sooner rather than later, that the suffering of the innocent at the hands of the patriarchy will end as soon as it possibly can, and that Gaia is restored before it is just too late.

A daughter bright

Alfrothul bears

ere Fenrir snatches her forth;

Her mother's paths

shall the maiden tread

When the gods to death have gone

- Vafþrúðnismál,[18] Stanza 47

Chapter 6 - References

1 *The Poetic Edda, Völuspá,* Henry Adams Bellows (translator), 1936, Evinity Publishing Inc.
2 K. Healy, L. McNally, G. Ruxtom et al., "Metabolic rate and body size are linked with perception of temporal information", *Animal Behavior*, 86 (4), October 2013, 685–696, accessed 27 May 2014 from http://dx.doi.org/10.1016/j.anbehav.2013.06.018
3 Ibid.
4 Nature, "What Plants Talk About", documentary film, 3 April 2013, accessed 27 May 2014 from http://www.pbs.org/wnet/nature/episodes/what-plants-talk-about/video-full-episode/8243/
5 Gareth Cook, "Do Plants Think", *Scientific American (5 June 2012),* accessed 24 May 2014 from http://www.scientificamerican.com/article.cfm?id=do-plants-think-daniel-chamovitz
6 Steve Mirsky, "Researcher Argues that Plants Can See", *Scientific American* (podcast), 26 June 2012, accessed 27 May 2014 from http://www.scientificamerican.com/podcast/episode.cfm?id=researcher-argues-that-plants-see-12-06-26
7 J. Cahill, Jr., G. McNickle, J. Haag et al., "Plants Integrate Information About Nutrients and Neighbors", *Science*, 25 June 2010, 328 (5986), p. 1657, doi: 10.1126/science.1189736
8 Murphy et al., "Kin recognition: Competition and cooperation in Impatiens (Balsaminaceae)", *American Journal of Botany*, 2009; 96 (11): 1990 DOI: 10.3732/ajb.0900006
9 O. Kostenko, T. Voorde, P. Mulder et al., "Legacy effects of aboveground-belowground interactions", *Ecology Letters*, 2012; DOI: 10.1111/j.1461-0248.2012.01801.x
10 Le Monde.fr, "Tricastin : une centrale sans failles?", Le Monde Planete, 22.07.2013, accessed 24 May 2014 from http://www.lemonde.fr/planete/article/2013/07/15/tricastin-une-centrale-sans-failles_3447959_3244.html
11 desmogblog.com, "Top 10 Facts About the Alberta Oil Sands", February 2014, accessed 27 May 2014 from http://www.desmogblog.com/top-10-facts-canada-alberta-oil-sands-information
12 M. Jenkins and B. Stirton, "Who Murdered the Virunga Gorillas?", *National Geographic* (July 2008), accessed 27 May 2014 from http://ngm.nationalgeographic.com/2008/07/virunga/jenkins-text
13 Sea Shepherd Conservation Society, website, accessed 13 February 2014 from http://www.seashepherd.org/cove-guardians/
14 J. Paungger und T. Poppe, "Das Mondjahr 2014", 29. April 2014
15 Trolljentas Verden, "Norwegische Trolle", accessed 24 May 2014 from http://www.trolljenta.no/kultur/trolle
16 A. Jarosz, "Iceland: Huldufólk", *National Geographic Traveler*, 10 April 2012, accessed 24 May 2014 from http://natgeotraveller.co.uk/blog/iceland-huldufolk/

17 World Health Organization, "WHO's first global report on antibiotic resistance reveals serious, worldwide threat to public health", 30 April 2014, accessed 30 May 2014 from http://www.who.int/mediacentre/news/releases/2014/amr-report/en/
18 *The Poetic Edda, Vafþrúðnismál*, Bellows

Chapter 7

Quantum Reality, Schrödinger's Capitalist, and Feminine Empowerment

The earth and the universe are filled with fundamental forces we cannot see, and even cannot explain, yet we encounter them and feel them and rely on them every moment of our existence. Gravity? Nope, not explained yet. Electricity/Magnetism? Explained only in and of itself, but not related to other forces. The Strong and Weak nuclear forces make the very atoms of our being what they are, but are little known and not fully understood. The search for a theory unifying all of these forces remains quixotic. The quantum universe, a universe filled with dimensions, is just as unseen by us, and even less understood than what we consider to be the fundamental forces of nature, yet the quantum universe is the *real* universe.

The four-dimensional (4D) "universe" of space and time with which we are so familiar is no more than a pseudo-universe with the rest of the universe filtered out. It is like taking a color movie with unimaginably great sound, turning it into a black-and-white movie with monaural sound, reducing it further into a black-and-white still picture, and then claiming this resulting black-and-white image is the original color movie. This is what happens when we take the "real-reality" of the quantum universe with all its dimensions and step it down to the level of 4D Physicality, and then believe the resulting faux-universe is the real thing.

Biologists studying the finest internal structures of bones are employing precisely the same methods and technologies as astrophysicists researching the largest structure in the universe: that of the observable universe's more than 1 billion galaxies. How can they do this? *The structure of the galaxies comprising the physical universe is identical to the internal structure of bone.*[1] Researchers studying neutrinos have turned their telescopes to monitoring whales. Among other significant findings, they discovered the previously unknown presence of sperm whales in the Mediterranean Sea. How could they do this? *Whales sing at the same wavelength as the neutrinos emitted by distant stars.*[2] These unexpected commonalities in extraordinarily disparate systems are no accident. They share structures and attributes because their underlying physics is identical.

It is just the same with quantum reality. From quantum entanglement to the double-slit experiment,[3] from the observer effect to retro-causality, quantum phenomena are very real, reasonably well understood and extensively researched by physicists, yet to most of us, they remain mysterious or even spooky, even though they are the quantum manifestations of the real, higher-dimensional (8D+) universe in our familiar 4D universe of space-time. Our universe *is* a quantum universe, but it has only been over the past few decades that physicists have begun to verify (and exploit) the quantum nature of our everyday, macroscopic world.

Time itself – our "clock time" - is a phenomenon that emerges from the seemingly bizarre but fundamental quantum concept of **entanglement**. Consider a very simple system arising from a photon. This photon is split into two photons which, being "born" from the same photon are now entangled – intimately interconnected in terms of their properties – regardless of the physical distance which separates them. These photons, we'll call them Alpha and Charlie, have a polarization, or "spin" - horizontal and vertical. What are the spins of Alpha and Charlie? In the quantum universe – *our* universe – *they exist in both spin states at the same time* (this is called **quantum superposition**). That is, until they are observed. Once observed, however, the **wave functions** of the photons collapse and we can determine their spins. But this really isn't the strangest part. What seems most amazing is that if we separate our photons by a large distance – say 18 km,[4] or 400 km,[5] or across the galaxy, or for that matter, across the universe – they remain intimately and inextricably linked, as if they are part of the same consciousness. Suppose Alpha and Charlie are separated by a very large distance, and we measure the spin of Alpha as vertical. If we independently observe Charlie's spin, we will find that it is horizontal, as if Charlie knows what Alpha's spin is and thus locks into the opposite spin. What's more is that the communication between Alpha and Charlie is truly instantaneous – at the moment Alpha's spin is observed and thus locked in, Charlie's spin is locked in, too. This communication between Alpha and Charlie is absolutely simultaneous – what Albert Einstein called "spooky action at a distance" ("spukhafte Fernwirkung").[6] We can even observe a photographic demonstration of entanglement in real-time.[7] The quantum fact of entanglement and instantaneous action at a distance, borne out during the past 40 years by many experiments over larger and larger distances at ever increasing sensitivities, seems to not just violate classical Newtonian mechanics ("how can particles interact if they do not *physically* interact?") but the relativistic restrictions placed by the speed of light ("how can particles seemingly communicate faster than the speed of light?"). This dilemma is only overcome when we admit that there is no violation of speed of light restrictions because quantum entanglement unfolds in a realm where clock time itself is meaningless. What or where is this "realm"? It is where we can observe – and *alter* - the universe of space-time (4D) from what physicists call a "god-like" perspective.

It is quantum entanglement that appears to be the fundamental, underlying phenomenon guiding the behavior of the universe. Time as we measure it on our clocks is a mere by-product of quantum entanglement. This is profound. The fact that time itself is "an emergent phenomenon that is a side effect of quantum entanglement"[8] should be as disconcerting to the powers-that-be as the rejection of geocentrism by Copernicus and Kepler was to the 16th century, and the unseating of Euclidean geometry, after being held for 2000 years as the only geometric system, was to the 19th century. For us who embrace our true Feeling selves, however, the realization that the universe is fundamentally about entanglement, about the intimate interconnection of everyone and everything, and furthermore that our interconnectedness is *not* imprisoned by 4D time, this realization is nothing short of exhilarating! The multitude of other bizarre quantum phenomena, no longer just theoretical concepts but also borne out by experiment, begin to fall into place. In **quantum retrocausality**, or backward causality, cause *follows* effect from the perspective of clock time – yes, time can run in reverse. Not only has retrocausality been demonstrated experimentally,[9] but entangled photons have been observed which never coexisted in the same timespan at all![10] Nor is all of this quantum entanglement restricted to systems of particles such as photons and electrons. Recent research has shown just how very fundamental the quantum universe in general, and quantum entanglement in particular, is to our very existence. Quantum entanglement has been demonstrated at room temperature for macroscopic solids,[11] is being shown to drive plant photosynthesis,[12] and accounts for the navigation of birds in the earth's magnetic field.[13] Perhaps most fundamentally of all, quantum entanglement appears to hold DNA itself together![14]

Even with the (often begrudging) acknowledgment of quantum reality growing over the past 100 or so years, patriarchy still has almost all of us convinced that the 4D pseudo-universe is not affected by quantum reality, but nothing could be further from the truth. There are many dimensions beyond 4D – so significant as to make the 4D reduced subset of dimensions a poor imitation of real-reality.¶ As far as "randomness" is concerned, that too is a strictly 4D phenomenon, but, as demonstrated by the **observer effect**, the quantum universe is not deterministic, either. It is quantum.

What is the "stuff" of this quantum realm that makes up the quantum universe, giving rise to all its quantum phenomena, and connects all of the universe's dimensions together, even our

---

¶   I am counting dimensions starting with a point in space which I call "0D". The three spatial dimensions (length, width, height, or put another way the {x,y,z} coordinate system) are "3D" and when clock-time t is added it is "4D", or space-time. This keeps with the usage in which time is referred to as the "fourth dimension".

familiar 4D ones? **Love.** Here's perhaps the simplest thing to say about the real, quantum universe and what it means for us:

> ***Love and Truth are a Unity.***
> ***This Unity is the ultimate reality,***
> ***from which all other realities emerge.***
> ***All of these realities are quantum.***

Nothing more nor less, but indeed nothing could be *more* than Love, and true Love has no sense of less, for it is unequivocal and complete.

Quantum chess on an infinite chessboard

Let's use a chessboard and chess pieces to model dimensionality and the quantum universe. Think of a chessboard consisting of alternating light and dark squares. There are normally 64 squares in an 8 X 8 grid, but our chessboard is a bit bigger – it is infinitely large. You are sitting on White's home side of the board (how one sits on the side of an infinite board is a question I'll leave unanswered). Let's use our chessboard as a model for the dimensions and the concept of dimensionality (Figure 7.1). What would 0D look like on this chessboard universe? It looks like the point defined by the intersection of the borders of each square. (If our universe were 0D it would be a trivial, boring one, but this

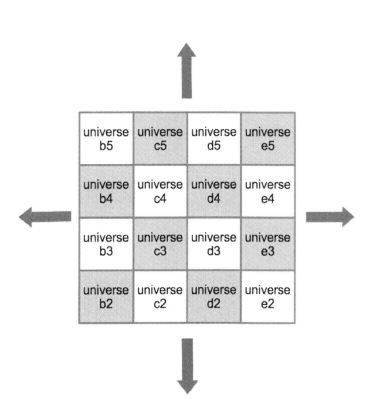

Figure 7.1 - The Infinite Chessboard

too is instructive, since this is kind of how our 4D "world" appears when observed from higher dimensional levels. More on this shortly). Each square on the chessboard is two-dimensional (2D), i.e. it has length and width, or an {x,y} coordinate system. Now imagine each square also has a height property, so the 2D squares on the chessboard now represent 3D space (the 2D square represents width, length, and height, or the {x,y,z} coordinate system). This covers three of our familiar four dimensions.

Each chessboard square represents a really *big* cube: each contains an entire physical universe, or in metaphysical terms, a 3D reality (in this book I use "universe" and "reality" interchangeably). Imagine one square near the middle of our infinite chessboard, say the square located at d4,[§] represents a small, isolated island and all of the people, flora and fauna inhabiting it, and all of the rocks and soils there too. This island is so isolated that as far as the inhabitants are concerned, the island and its surrounding seas are their entire universe, they've never had any contact with anyone from anywhere else. The 3D spaces represented by the squares nearby d4 (c4, e4, d3, d5, c3, e3, c5, e5) look very similar to d4, but there are small differences. The 3D universe represented by the adjacent square e4 has a small cottage on a bluff overlooking the ocean on the south side of the island, whereas it is an unsettled place on d4. The adjacent c4 square/universe looks just like d4, except in the c4 universe a

---

[§] there is a standardized so-called "algebraic" notation for denoting chess piece positions on the board in which rows are represented by numbers and the columns by letters, starting with "a1" at White's lower left corner.

family of hedgehogs live on the bluff, but in the d4 and e4 universes there are rabbits there. Each of the squares in a row represent a different universe/reality, with the squares adjacent to a given square being very similar to the universe you're in, and the universes being increasingly different as you move away from your square. When you consider squares very distant from your d4 square, the island-universe looks quite different: in some distant squares (e.g. q15) the island is uninhabited, in other distant squares (e.g. a1) our island is an overpopulated, polluted mess.

Two Kinds of Time

We are still missing an important dimension – time. Introducing time makes our model more realistic but adds complexity, too. When we add the time dimension, each chessboard square now represents 4D space-time, i.e. width, length, height, and time, or the $\{x,y,z,t\}$ coordinate system. (note: when I speak of "Physicality" in this book I am speaking of 4D space-time, thus including time in Physicality.) Remember, each square represents a complete universe in 4D space-time.

We can symbolically represent the universe of square d4 as $\{x_{d4}, y_{d4}, z_{d4}, t_{d4}\}$, that of square c3 as $\{x_{c3}, y_{c3}, z_{c3}, t_{c3}\}$, and so on. Within each of these universes, "time" means our ordinary experience of **clock time**, as well as all of the manifestations of special relativity and general relativity.

Our familiar "clock time", t, is a mere by-product of quantum entanglement. Within each square "universe" on our chessboard, clock time, t, ticks on, and on. You could imagine each 4D universe of space-time having a kind of master clock ensuring time always runs in one direction (forward), effect always follows cause, and nothing appears to happen faster than the limitations of the speed of light. Note that there is no connection between the clock time of the 4D universe of one square vs. that of another square (e.g. $t_{d4} \neq t_{d3} \neq t_{c4}$ etc.) In each of these 4D universes, time behaves in what is called a space-like manner, i.e. the time dimension, t, behaves just like the other spatial dimensions x, y, and z.

At this point, however, we must divorce ourselves from our ordinary sense of clock-time, t, or even from a sense of time wedded to special relativity. In our real, quantum universe, there are *two kinds of time at work*. This second kind of time I'll call **absolute time**, representing it as τ. This τ-time is the kind of time which applies when you look at a 4D universe *from the outside,* as shown in Figure 7.2. When we take the perspective of absolute time, τ, all of the quantum phenomena we observe from *within* a 4D universe (e.g. quantum entanglement, retrocausality, the double-slit experiment, the observer effect) fall into place. The predictions of theoretical physicists are consistently borne out by experimental results: clock time, t, is *not* in any way a fundamental concept but is "emergent" from, that is to say a by-product of, quantum entanglement. Most

$\tau5$	x_{c5} y_{c5} z_{c5} t_{c5}	x_{d5} y_{d5} z_{d5} t_{d5}	x_{e5} y_{e5} z_{e5} t_{e5}
$\tau4$	x_{c4} y_{c4} z_{c4} t_{c4}	x_{d4} y_{d4} z_{d4} t_{d4}	x_{e4} y_{e4} z_{e4} t_{e4}
$\tau3$	x_{c3} y_{c3} z_{c3} t_{c3}	x_{d3} y_{d3} z_{d3} t_{d3}	x_{e3} y_{e3} z_{e3} t_{e3}

Figure 7.2 - The infinite chessboard populated by 4D space-time universes/realities. The t within each square "universe" is *clock time*. The rows of *absolute time*, τ , are fixed, and they are external to the chessboard.

experiments demonstrating this have been conducted with laboratory "toy universes", which begs the question, can we access the perspective of a "god-like observer" such that we take ourselves *outside* of the 4D universe and all its restrictions?[§] Though whenever physicists and engineers test or use quantum phenomena they are doing exactly this, the extraordinarily tantalizing applied science is still in its infancy. We could wait around for the hard science to catch up ... or we can just be the creator goddesses we already are, and go ahead and create the Truth-based, Love-based universe we want and deserve!

Let us return to our infinite chessboard. Recall that each square represents a 4D universe of space-time. Within each square, that is within each universe/reality, in addition to the dimensions of length, width, and height there is a time dimension, t, which is like that of a running clock, but behaves essentially like the other spatial dimensions (in fact we can call it 4D "space"). This "clock time", t, may be our ordinary waking experience of time, or it can be warped or dilated as predicted by special and general relativity, but it does *not* account for the behavior of quantum phenomena. In fact, these quantum phenomena should be *impossible* from the standpoint of the time (t) of space-time. Yet quantum phenomena *are* real, just as real as special and general relativity, or evolution, or human-caused global warming. Quantum phenomena are not just

---

§   When we look at the 4D universe of space-time from the external "god-like perspective", time appears static, as predicted by the Wheeler-DeWitt equation, what physicists call "the problem of time". Remarkably, this fact is supported by recent experiments.

observed in our 4D space-time universe, experimental evidence shows they are essential for the very functioning of our 4D universe/reality. What is going on? When we introduce absolute time, τ, all of these quantum phenomena make sense, but that leads to the inescapable conclusion that absolute τ-time exists outside of our 4D universe. This perspective fully supports the notion of the "multiverse", an infinite collection of 4D universes, as represented by each square on our infinite chessboard.

Absolute time, τ, is fixed to the chessboard itself, and is represented by each horizontal row of the chessboard (e.g. τ_4 would be the absolute (τ) time of horizontal row 4, τ_3 the absolute time of row 3, etc., as shown in Figure 7.2). You could say that from the τ - perspective, you know everything there is to know about a given 4D universe, or put actively, when you have the perspective of absolute time you have creative control over which 4D universe you "live in" or experience. From the perspective of τ - time there is no "forward" or "backward", either. Absolute time does not preferentially "run", say, from τ_3 to τ_4, absolute τ - time does not "run" at all! This accounts for clock-time, t, seeming to run "backwards" (e.g. quantum retrocausality, in which cause follows from effect) or seemingly running "sideways" (e.g. the double-slit experiment, where a single particle moves through two slits at exactly the same time).

These very real observations of quantum phenomena do not mean clock-time within a 4D universe is somehow misbehaving. There is something much more profound going on.

These phenomena mean we are changing 4D space-time universes! We can think of the case of retrocausality as a move "backward" on the chessboard (towards us, along a column), say from square d4 to square d3, and hence from absolute-time τ_4 to absolute-time τ_3. The double-slit experiment represents a sideways move on our chessboard (parallel to us, left or right across a row), say from square d4 to c4, or d4 to e4. In this case, absolute-time remains fixed at τ_4 but we move to a kind of "parallel" universe. But how do we gain control over which universe, over which reality, we live in? How do we loose ourselves from the bonds of space-time within a given 4D universe? It is one thing to sit contemplating an infinite chessboard populated by infinite universes, but how do we actually *move* from one square to another? How do we change our reality?

Schrödinger's Capitalist

Sadly, this is what so many of us have been taught by patriarchy and their minions is supposed to be our "comfortable" reality:

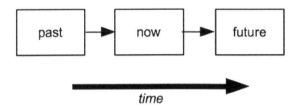

Figure 7.3 - Dreadful Determinism

Nonsense! We don't live in a universe/reality like this, and it would be a meaningless one, not to mention ridiculously boring, if we did. Completely and utterly deterministic, Figure 7.3 describes a faux-universe of deception and enslavement, with no chance of creating the reality we want, and the only hope of exit lying in a concocted "afterlife". Mercifully, this does not describe reality.

Our real reality is much more like that of Figure 7.4, an interpretation of the well known "Schrödinger's Cat" paradox[§]. I am a cat lover, however, so I'm going to change the narrative a little bit and call it "Schrödinger's Capitalist". This paradox places a capitalist in a box with a high explosive, a radioactive atom, and a Geiger counter. There is a 50% chance the atom will decay radioactively, in which case the Geiger counter detects the decay and triggers the explosive, killing the capitalist. There is also a 50% chance the atom will not decay at all, sparing the pathetic bloke. The wave nature of the radioactive atom's decay, and the quantum nature of reality (i.e. quantum superposition) means, however, that the atom is *both* decayed *and* not-decayed until an observer opens the box. By extension, this means our unfortunate capitalist is both alive *and* dead until we open the lid and observe his state. Once we do this the wave function collapses, and each of the two states is precipitated in time (clock time, t). Note that I am saying *each of the two states occurs*, not just one-state (decayed atom, dead capitalist) or the other state (non-decayed atom, undead capitalist). Through the act of simply peering into the box and observing the state of the capitalist we have moved from one universe, represented by square d4 on our chessboard, where the capitalist is both alive *and* dead, to two new universes, d3, in which he is alive, and d5,

---

§   Schrödinger never intended his paradox to be an argument *for* the quantum universe, he meant it to demonstrate the seeming absurdity of quantum reality. His paradox has been borne out by experiment, however, and Schrödinger's name has unwittingly become identified with supporting the very quantum theory he decried. So you see the universe has a great sense of humor and poetic justice.

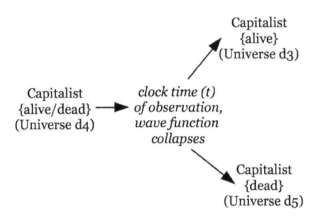

Figure 7.4 - Schrödinger's Capitalist

in which our capitalist has shuffled off his mortal coil.[15] The universes of squares d3, d4, and d5 all exist, they are equally real. For that matter, all of the universes on our quantum chessboard are real universes. It is through the collapse of the wave function that we move from one universe/reality "square" on the chessboard to another. But in which universe do we wind up? Recall the radioactive atom had a 50% chance of decaying or not decaying. Likewise, we have a 50% chance of winding up in the universe of d3 where the capitalist can continue to torment us, and a 50% chance of achieving universe d5 where we are freed from his shackles. The key concept here is that we, the observer, bring about the collapse of the wave function deciding the capitalist's fate: *there is no wave function collapse independent of us observing the system in question.* There is no escaping our participation, no matter how hard we might try. The unfortunate part is that this is exactly how many of us allow or reality to unfold: unwittingly letting chance collapse the wave functions of our lives, or worse, ceding the collapse of these wave functions to someone else. The net effect of either of these is the same – we are not the ones determining our universe/reality.

We have three choices:

(1) We can let things run like Schrödinger's Capitalist, effectively allowing the flip of a coin or the roll of a die to determine how life "happens" to us.

(2) We can hand control over to someone else and let them choose our reality for us.

(3) *We* can choose into which square our wave function collapses, i.e. we can choose our universe/reality, or at the very least, we can greatly alter the probability of which universe/reality we move to in our favor (if we could revise the conditions of Schrödinger's Capitalist to a 99% probability of the atom decaying, wouldn't we want to do that?).

Regardless of which of these three choices we make:

There is no independent reality without us.

Whether we choose to admit it or not, we are not just active *participants* in the universe, we are *creators*, each of us a creator-goddess in our own right. Not only that, but we are *infinitely* empowered creators, each of us, because we have the universe, the quantum universe, and all of its cohesive, synergistic interconnectedness at our disposal. We do exercise our creative power, always, whether we realize it, or admit it, or not. It is our *choice* if we exercise that power as a mere "observer". With option (1), we create our reality, but it is a passive creation, just like the "observer" peering into Schrödinger's box. Those who choose option (2) are the myrmidons and minions of patriarchy and the archons. In either of these cases we are passive, and in both of these cases we remain trapped in mentality, bound to someone else's mental constructs and the pseudo-reality patriarchy has created for us. How then do we achieve option (3)? How do we intentionally create the reality we want, *deliberately* moving to, or at least greatly increase the probability of moving to, a universe/reality "square" that is not just different, but far, *far better*? How do we and the other good people of the world make it so that we *will* find each other and that we *do* create a universe/reality of Love, Truth, and Goddess?

Feminine Empowerment

In order to deliberately move on our chessboard, we need a chess piece. Since we can choose our piece, let's pick a Queen, the most powerful, flexible chess piece available (is it any accident that the King is the least powerful, most inflexible piece?). Let's place our queen on square (universe/reality) d4. We, the chess player, control our queen's movement with our free will. This does not happen at the level of Physicality (4D space-time). Physicality is what happens *within* a chessboard square. The Mentality "box" never even enters into our creation process; it is a three-dimensional space (5, 6, and 7D) ancillary to the creation we exercise with our true free will. In our quantum chess model, we truly create when we pick up our queen and deliberately move her to another square on the chessboard. We take this action using our free will based on our true Feelings. We create in the realm of Feelingality, 8D+. When we take baby steps we move our queen to an adjacent square. We occasionally may move our queen directly to a more distant square, but that is not as easy (think of a chessboard populated by other chess pieces on intervening squares between our current universe/reality and a more distant one). When we move in concert with the other good people of the world, that is when we engage in a dance with their chess pieces so that we all reach the universe/realities we want to reach. No matter what move we make, whether a baby step to an adjacent square or a more radical move to a more distant one, whenever we exercise our free will and deliberately move in true Feeling, *we take a quantum leap*. Whenever we take a quantum leap, we engage the *entire* quantum universe.

We truly exercise our free will, we truly create, when we create from our true Feeling in the 8D+ realm of Feelingality. *This is Feminine Empowerment*. Patriarchy and their minions cannot create this way - they have no access to their true Feelings because they've cut themselves off from them. What passes for "creating" in their pseudo-universe is a feeble, nefarious imitation of our own. This is why patriarchy fears us - they know (or at least can sense) that we have access to true Feminine creation, creation that comes from true Feeling, quantum creation. Our creation is infinitely more powerful than anything they could concoct.

True Creation is Feminine Empowerment

Feminine Empowerment, true creation, is flexible in its firmness, and it is firm in its flexibility. Feminine empowerment is always done for what is right, because it is always born in true Feeling, it is always based on the unity of Love and Truth. Feminine empowerment can be no other way. Feminine empowerment means us creating together, in harmony with the quantum universe and with each other. When we create our universe/reality with Feminine empowerment, there are never losers, we are each of us harmonious winners. We all are guaranteed to win through peaceful, Truth-based, Love-based, Goddess-centered creation. Using our true Feelings, implemented with our intuition, exercising our free will, we have *limitless* power to create a universal reality, a Feminine reality, that is itself one of Love and Truth. We don't cede our power to someone else, letting them move our queen for us, nor do we entrust the movement of our queen to mere random chance. When we engage our true Feelings in Love and Truth, when we use our intuition to actively and deliberately *create* our universe, *we* are the creators, we move our queen in concert with the other good people of the world to a universe/reality of *our* choosing. We know the square we move to, the universe/reality we create, will always be a fairer one, a better one, eventually a great one, because we are creating with Feminine Empowerment.

In our final chapter, we will explore what it means to "Just Say Fuck It!" to patriarchy, to say "Fuck It!" to fear, and to cast off all of patriarchy's mental constructs and pseudo-realities, and actively create *our* reality, a quantum reality of Goddess!

Chapter 7 - References

1 Projekt Zukunft, "Im Inneren der Knochen", *Deutsche Welle*, 28.02.2014, accessed on 12 March 2014 from http://dw.de/p/1BGIJ

2 ASPERA, "Listening to Whales with Neutrino Telescopes", *Interactions.org Particle Physics News and Resources*, 25 November 2010, accessed on 15 March 2014 from http://www.interactions.org/cms/?pid=1030250

3 Roger Bach, Damian Pope, Sy-Hwang Liou and Herman Batelaan, "Controlled double-slit electron diffraction", *New J. Phys.* (**15**) 033018, 13 March 2013, accessed 17 March 2014 from doi:10.1088/1367-2630/15/3/033018

4 D. Salart, A. Baas, J. A. W. van Houwelingen et al., "Spacelike Separation in a Bell Test Assuming Gravitationally Induced Collapses", *Phys. Rev. Lett.* (100) 220404, 6 June 2008, accessed 15 March 2014 from http://journals.aps.org/prl/abstract/10.1103/PhysRevLett.100.220404

5 M. Zhang, "Scientists May Do Quantum Entanglement Test with a 400nm Nikon Lens on the ISS", *Petapixel*, 10 April 2013, accessed on 14 March 2014 from http://petapixel.com/2013/04/10/scientists-may-do-quantum-entanglement-test-with-a-400mm-nikon-lens-on-the-iss/

6 "Einsteins spukhafte Fernwirkung erstmals auf Kamera", *uni:view Magazin*, 29. Mai 2013, accessed 14 March 2014 from http://medienportal.univie.ac.at/uniview/forschung/detailansicht/artikel/einsteins-spukhafte-fernwirkung-erstmals-auf-kamera/

7 Robert Fickler, Mario Krenn, Radek Lapkiewicz et al., "Real-time Imaging of Quantum Entanglement", *Scientific Reports* (3) 1914, 29 May 2013, accessed 15 March 2014 from http://www.nature.com/srep/2013/130529/srep01914/pdf/srep01914.pdf

8 The Physics arXiv blog, "Quantum Experiment Shows How Time 'Emerges' from Entanglement." *Medium.* accessed on 15 March 2014 from https://medium.com/the-physics-arxiv-blog/d5d3dc850933

9 Xiao-song Ma, Steffan Zotter, Johannes Kofler et al., "Experimental delayed-choice entanglement swapping", *Nature Physics* (8), 479-484 (2012), accessed on 15 March 2014 from doi:10.1038/nphys2294

10 E. Megidish, A. Halevy, T. Shacham et al., "Entanglement Swapping between Photons that have Never Coexisted", *Phys. Rev. Lett.* (110) 210403, 22 May 2013, accessed 15 March 2014 from http://journals.aps.org/prl/abstract/10.1103/PhysRevLett.110.210403

11 "Entangling Macroscopic Diamonds at Room Temperature", Science (334) 6060, 2 December 2011, accessed 14 February 2014 from http://www.sciencemag.org/content/334/6060/1253.full

12 DOE/Lawrence Berkeley National Laboratory, "Untangling the quantum entanglement behind photosynthesis", *Science Daily*, 11 May 2010, accessed 15 March 2014 from http://www.sciencedaily.com/releases/2010/05/100510151356.htm

13 I. K. Kominis, "Quantum Zeno Effect Underpinning the Radical-Ion-Pair Mechanism of Avian Magnetoreception", *arXiv.org*, 16 April 2008, accessed 14 March 2014 from arXiv:0804.2646

14 "Quantum Entanglement Holds DNA together, Say Physicists", *MIT Technology Review*, 28 June 2010, accessed 14 March 2014 from, http://www.technologyreview.com/view/419590/quantum-entanglement-holds-dna-together-say-physicists/

15 William Shakespeare, *Hamlet*, Act III

Chapter 8

Just Say Fuck It!
(Creating Our Reality)

We are the good people of the world. We *are* finding each other and we *are* bringing about the change that only Love brings. We embrace the Feminine, and we *are* the Feminine. We embrace Goddess. We *are* Goddess.

We are "Just Saying Fuck It!" to patriarchy. We are saying "Fuck It!" to patriarchy's oppression and repression, and we mean it. To say "Fuck It!" means not worrying about outcomes, not living in fear, not caring what anyone else thinks, and taking risks for what we *know* is right. The supposed "risks" we take? It is us embracing our true-selves, the creator-selves we really are. We know what is the right thing to do because we *feel* what is right. Our true Feelings never fail us because they arise in the Love and Truth of Goddess, and our intuition never fails us because it arises in our true Feelings. When we say "Fuck It!" to living in the dysfunctional and dystopian prison patriarchy has engineered for us, Goddess is unchained. When we take action using our intuition, the prison gates are flung open, and Goddess is liberated! As soon as we are outside of that woeful place, we realize that their prison never had any chains or walls or gates in the first place!

The destruction wrought by patriarchy is all too real, but their imprisoning pseudo-reality is not. We always had the freedom to simply walk out of their horrid mental construct whenever we liked. It was just a matter of exercising our free will by saying and *meaning* "Fuck It!", putting one foot in front of the other, and leaving their prison - forever. When we and others like us *do* walk out of bondage into the azure skies of Truth, Goddess is loosed upon earth. With Goddess unleashed, Love takes root and begins to grow. Love is Feminine, She is fertile, and She begins to grow *everywhere*. As more and more of us embrace the Feminine and unite in Goddess, we soon see those prison walls crumble in Her soft, warm, nurturing embrace. We see that the combination of Love and Truth is unstoppable just as Goddess is unstoppable. Goddess is Liberated!

Creating our Reality

We are, each and every one of us, most powerful creators. Our power is nothing less than creating our own Goddess-based, Love-based, Truth-based reality. Each of us is an immensely powerful creator-goddess in our own right, and our united power is unimaginable. You can see why patriarchy fears us. Far more importantly, do you see why Gaia and all of Her life embrace us? We have the very power to restore Goddess to earth, to reclaim our reality, to heal Gaia, and to re-establish a reality of Truth and Love! Wow!

In the previous chapter we saw how the universe is a quantum universe, and how that quantum universe is not some esoteric concept but the very engine which drives our reality, including our 4D experience of reality. The seemingly bizarre quantum phenomena our physicists observe, are a mere tip of the iceberg of what quantum reality is and what it really means to us. It is a very good thing that we don't have to understand quantum reality and processes in any mental way in order to harness the power of the quantum universe, for just like the Dyads trying to comprehend 3D, it will always remain outside of our mental grasp. But our feeling-self, our true, *real-self*, she understands quantum reality perfectly, and she knows just how to use it!

Our Creation Process

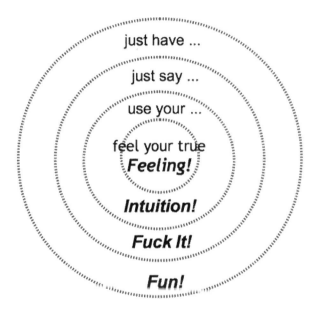

Figure 8.1 - Creating Our Reality

*Our feeling-self, our creator-self, she **is** quantum.*

Think of the layers of the sun, kind of like the layers of an onion (see Figure 8.1). When we **feel our true feelings**, this is like the central core of the sun, where fusion takes place. Just as this innermost solar layer is the source for all of the sun's energy,[1] this is our "power layer" which drives everything else in our creation process. Your true Feelings are a unity, the fusion of Love and Truth, your fusion with Goddess. Just as the sun's core is powered by myriad tiny fusion reactions, so is our creation process powered by our myriad baby steps. These myriad processes, these countless baby steps, interconnect in an intricate quantum network that generates our reality. All that we do, every little, individual thing, every baby step that derives from our true Feelings, all fuse and interweave in a massive network of inexhaustible creative synergy. The sun's core is the ultimate creative force of our entire physical world; our true Feeling-self is the ultimate creative force of our universal reality.

Though what we create at the level of true Feeling, in Feelingality, is a most real reality, it does not yet exist in our 4D experience. It is when we **use our intuition** to take action and do what we know is right, because we truly *feel* it is right, that we are able to create a 4D physical reality to match the 8D+ reality

---

1   http://www.spacestationinfo.com/layers-sun.htm

our true selves have already created. Our intuition is like the next solar layer outward, the radiative zone. This is where our true Feelings "radiate" into our creation process. This "radiation" is our intuition. Our intuition is the conduit between our feeling-self which "lives" in the higher dimensional (8D+) reality of our true-self and the physical (4D) "reality" (pseudo-reality) of our ordinary waking experience.

The third layer out, modeled by the sun's convective zone, is where we **_Just Say Fuck It!_** We achieve tranquility when we are compassionate to ourselves. To "Just Say Fuck It!" is to stop beating ourselves up, and to just do what is right, because it is right. Fuck patriarchy's threatened consequences. This will cause turbulence in our lives, and this is an area of much turbulence on the sun, too. When we truly create, our creation process must create turbulence. We are taking down patriarchy's status quo! We are dismantling patriarchy's pseudo-reality. Without going through this turbulence, there would be no illumination, no wisdom, no abundance, no real peace, and no real joy, either. The convective zone is the first layer of the sun we are able to see (manifesting visually in the sun's photosphere), and likewise it is when we say "Fuck It!" that our creation process really manifests as 4D physical reality. When we just say "Fuck It!" the imprisoning veil we've acquiesced to living under is rent, and we feel our true Feelings and recognize our intuition in 4D. When we say "Fuck It!" we are no longer just creating in the 8D+ reality of Feelingality, nor are we just *potentially* creating in our waking 4D world via our intuition, but we are *actually creating in 4D*, in everyday space-time. It is thus when we just say "Fuck It!" that we achieve real abundance, and finally reach the safe, soft embrace of the reality of Goddess.

To "Just Say Fuck It!" is to be true to ourselves. It is really shorthand for "just *say* 'Fuck It!' and *mean* 'Fuck It!' and *do* 'Fuck It!'" For example, it is saying "Fuck It!" when you talk about exercising, or eating well, or quitting a job that is killing you, or saying someone should do something about the gross injustices in the world. It is meaning "Fuck It!" when you sincerely intend to exercise, eat well, quit your job, or get really riled up about those injustices. It is quite another thing entirely, though, to truly *do* "Fuck It!", to say "to hell with you and your opinions patriarchy, and to hell with the fears you feed us and the baggage you saddle us with, I'm actually getting out for a daily walk, I'm not eating your processed foods that are slowly killing me, and I'm quitting that horrid job that I *know* is killing me even when I have no *idea* what I'll do next, because I know with the greatest certainty that I am taking all of these actions with the full strength of the quantum universe, of Goddess Herself, supporting me." It is willfully blind to deny earth's climate crisis. It is saying "Fuck It!" when we recognize there *is* a climate crisis. It is meaning "Fuck It!" when you become outraged about the wanton destruction of Gaia. It is *doing* "Fuck It!", when you actually get rid of your car and deal with the resulting hardships because it is the right thing to do for the planet. When you are an LGBTQ person, it is willful blindness to deny it. It is saying "Fuck It!" when you recognize and admit to yourself you are LGBTQ. It is meaning "Fuck It!" and doing "Fuck It!" when you live openly as the LGBTQ person you are, no matter what it might mean to your relationships with your family, or friends, or to your job. (If your friends and family are truly friends and family, they will happily embrace and support you. If your job is the right one for you, it won't matter one bit if you are LGBTQ).

And what about the "abundance" and sustenance one so often hears about, particularly from the preachers of the "new age movement"? We only generate *real* abundance and sustenance when we say "Fuck It!" and mean "Fuck It!" and do "Fuck It!". Doing "Fuck It!" is taking deliberate action in our lives. No good can ever result by compromise with patriarchy, and no good can ever result from accepting any of their pseudo-earth's pseudo-realities. We can never be the 4D manifestation of our real-self, we can never truly create anything, whenever we make any kind of compromise with patriarchy whatsoever.

We can achieve nothing real by working within their system. Complete exercise of our free will, adhering only to the real-reality of our own true Feeling-self, is the only way to live and flourish in a Feminine reality, the reality of Goddess. Much more often than not, however, we cannot take massive action in our lives, but we can take many deliberate baby steps. Like the multitude of tiny fusion reactions within the sun, our quantum universe thrives on baby steps. Almost everything that happens in the universe originates with a small step, a small perturbation, a small disruption in space-time. Baby steps are the nature of things, and they are how we create our reality. Picking up litter, drying your clothes in the sunshine, riding your bicycle, taking public transit, buying and eating non-GMO, locally and fairly grown food, reusing and repurposing what you have, recycling when you must, respecting the plants and animals who give their lives for your sustenance, buying new things only when you absolutely must, and when you do, ensuring they were produced with minimal environmental impact and maximum benefit to those who produced them, better still, giving to and sharing with others ... each of these seemingly inconsequential acts, and a multitude of acts just like them, really *do* matter in the "grand scheme of things". They not only make a difference, *they are the difference!* It is with just such tiny changes that revolutions happen. There is a universal synergy at work here, and this is a quantum synergy.

Consider the physical example of a cascade of particles that develops when a gamma ray hits the earth's upper atmosphere (Figure 8.2). One seemingly inconsequential high energy particle collision unleashes astounding energy, and spawns a cascade of myriad particles. Likewise, one single baby step in *doing* what is right, a baby step that is based on the Truth and Love of your true Feeling, and which arises from the certainty of your intuition derived from that true Feeling, this kind of baby step, just like the gamma ray, has incredibly high "energy" and launches a cascade of reactions and true change throughout the universe. Our creative power may start in baby steps, but the result is massive!

Figure 8.2 - Artist conception of a cosmic ray shower (ASPERA/Novapix/L.Bret).

Finally, it is in the outermost layer of the sun where the sun interacts with the rest of the solar system. In our Creation Process this is the layer where we **have fun!** Our "have fun!" layer derives its "energy" and support from the three layers within it. To "have fun!" is intimately tied with just saying, meaning, and doing "Fuck It!" Having fun in times of adversity or difficulty, or in the face of overwhelming "odds" purporting to be against your success, this is the hallmark of *truly* being in touch with the real you, and trusting in the Truth of the quantum universe (something the *Tao Te Ching* emphasizes repeatedly). To "have fun!" in the face of all the noise and discouragement we are assaulted with is no small feat, more so when we realize just how consequential all that we do really is. The problem is, if we don't "have fun!", if we take things all too seriously, we stifle our creation process just as it is blossoming. While writing this book, whenever I thought "oh shit! I am writing a book!", I started to become concerned with things like "how will my book be received? What if it doesn't sell? What will the critics and trolls say and how can I preemptively respond to them?" and quite quickly my own creative process ground to a halt. When I just wrote with an attitude of "Fuck it! This is *my* book, I know what I am writing is *my* Truth, And I am having fun! I don't give a damn what critics or trolls say..." then the writing just flowed, and the book, as other authors have remarked, fairly "wrote itself".

By the way, we need not worry about patriarchy co-opting our creation process and employing it against us. Remember, the engine of our creation process is true Feeling, and patriarchy has no access to true Feeling whatsoever. They are forever wedded to, and mired in, the box of mentality, and remember that mentality has no role in our creation process. Neither should we ever beat ourselves up for any "bad" decision we've made in the past, nor for not doing more than we perhaps did do. Quantum causality runs forward *and* backward in time; the quantum universe pays no attention to the direction of clock time.

Not only can we undo damage, we can erase it, wipe it out, and shift our reality. (The only ones who should feel badly are patriarchy and their minions who have done dreadful things to us and to Gaia. Alas, they never will).

Our true feelings are *always* valid, and our baby steps are *always* effective. Our creation process *always* works. Our quantum universe ensures this, and like the shower of particles precipitated by a single gamma ray, one small baby step creates a cascade of positive change we could scarcely imagine. There are those rare occasions when we do make large "quantum jumps", and we should rightly congratulate ourselves when we take those leaps, but far more often it is our quantum baby steps that yield enormous impact. It is one thing to talk about taking ourselves out of the game and not compromising anymore, but doing it? That is where we are truly courageous. It may seem like a paradox, but when we are courageous in our firmness, when we take action and *do* what we know is right heedless of patriarchy's threats, it is *then* that we are truly having fun! When we just "have fun!" we are enjoying what we do, no matter how seemingly serious what we do, or what we refuse to do, appears to be. It is humorous when one hears the well-meaning advice "give yourself permission to have fun". What does that mean? You give yourself permission and then wait for fun to happen? That's laughable! The way to "have fun!" is to *just have fun*, to actively do it! Fun is something that you must experience, you cannot sit around waiting for it to come to you. When we "have fun!" patriarchy has completely lost us. When we have fun we smile and there is a spring in our step. It is like the giddy feeling you get when you embrace your lover and close the bedroom door behind you. It is when we "have fun!" that we fully assimilate our creative power. The chains are loosed, the fear is gone, and from us the most profound, glorious, joyous, unstoppable empowerment, blooms and blossoms and explodes!

Goddess Liberated

Goddess is astonishingly clear, yet She defies definition

Goddess is ineffable, yet every moment that we *feel*, we feel Her intimately

Goddess is transcendent

Goddess is Feminine, and She is *the* Feminine

Goddess is empowerment: *Feminine Empowerment*

Goddess is Love, and Truth, and *Love and Truth are inseparable*

Goddess is deeply within each of us

Goddess is *Feeling*

Goddess is Physicality. She is *not* mentality,
nor is She materialism.

Goddess is *quantum*

Goddess is the *universe*. Our universe is quantum.

Goddess is the space between matter,
and the space between anti-matter

Goddess is everywhere

Goddess is fun!

Goddess is *Gaia*. Goddess is Her earth
and all of earth's creatures.

Goddess is *unity*

Goddess is honest

Goddess is atheistic. Goddess is *not* god.

Goddess is *never* to be worshipped,
nor is She to be prayed to

Goddess does *not* judge, nor does She ever punish us

Goddess' Love is unconditional

Goddess is complete individual responsibility

Goddess is firmness in flexibility, and flexibility in firmness

Goddess is true yin and true yang, and She is the Tao

Goddess is uncompromising in Her integrity

Goddess is unstoppable

Goddess is our Mother

Goddess completely embraces us and She is always with us. We are never alone.

Goddess is protection. Goddess is support. Goddess is encouragement. She cheers us on! Goddess is the warmest embrace and the tenderest caress.

Goddess is our truest friend, and She is our most passionate lover

Goddess is orgasm!

Goddess is *us*: the Feminine us

You could go on and on about Goddess and never tire, but you could never come close to describing who or what Goddess is with any kind of completeness

Goddess is boundless

Yet each of us in our true selves - that is, in our Feeling, Feminine selves – each of us knows Goddess, and we know her intimately. We know *exactly* who She is.

We are Goddess when we truly Love, and when we are Loved!

Goddess **is**

and yes ...

Goddess is Liberated!

Just Say Fuck It! (Creating Our Reality)

Goddess Liberated

Index

Acknowledgments

My most heartfelt love and thanks go to my family for their extraordinary support and encouragement throughout the entire creation process of this work, extending from nascent thoughts put to paper beginning in 2008, through the writing of this book as a book for the past year, and all of their true feelings in reading, feedback, and editing support. I could never have written this book without them!

I also want to express my special gratitude to Anna Hasenaka for her extraordinary work on the cover art, which was outstanding from more than 400 submitted designs. Her concept captures the essence and spirit of this book in a beautiful abstract picture. It was a true pleasure working with her throughout the design process.

Goddess Liberated

About the Author

Ariadne Ross' extensive study of ethics, social economics, physics and metaphysics has spanned more than three decades. Fluent in English and German, her extraordinarily diverse career includes work as an engineer, statistician, military officer, and musician, enabling her to experience the full range of depths - and heights - of human behavior.

Ariadne has published numerous articles in academic journals in science and engineering, and she has taught diverse classes ranging from calculus and computer programming to ethics, project management, and music theory and performance. She is an accomplished pianist and cellist, and is an *I Ching* master. *Goddess Liberated* is Ariadne's first book.

30934258R10132

Made in the USA
Charleston, SC
30 June 2014